Ciao Italia Pronto!

Also by Mary Ann Esposito

Ciao Italia Pronto!

30-MINUTE RECIPES
FROM AN ITALIAN KITCHEN

Mary Ann Esposito

St. Martin's Press   New York

Color photographs copyright © 2005 by Chris Vaccaro
Black-and-white photographs copyright © 2005 by Paul Lally

www.stmartins.com

Design by Phil Mazzone

Library of Congress Cataloging-in-Publication Data

Esposito, Mary Ann.
    Ciao Italia pronto! : 30-minute recipes from an Italian kitchen / Mary Ann Esposito.—1st ed.
        p. cm.
    ISBN 0-312-33908-9
    EAN 978-0-312-33908-1
    1. Cookery, Italian. 2. Quick and easy cookery. I. Title.

TX723.E8699 2005
641.5'55'0945—dc22

                                                                                            2005051209

First Edition: October 2005

10   9   8   7   6   5   4   3   2   1

For Beth, Jennifer, and Christopher,
the new generation of good cooks

If Italian cookbooks do not wish to deceive their readers they should start out with these words. Obtain the best of ingredients, as fresh as they can be found, and within the bounds of skill, preserve their identity in the preparation. Thus forewarned, the reader could attain not only the true cooking of Italy, *la vera cucina Italiana*, but a deep understanding of Italy and the Italians.

—Luigi Barzini, *The Cooking of Italy*

Contents

Acknowledgments

The concept for this book belongs to so many. I am grateful to the following who have guided me in the direction of this work. My husband, Guy, who is always my best fan and critic and who can often predict what is on the food horizon sooner than I can. To the staff of St. Martin's Press, especially my editor, Michael Flamini, a passionate and innovative cook in his own right, for his advice, enthusiasm, and attention to detail in guiding me in this project. To editorial assistant Katherine Tiernan for keeping me on schedule. To Steve Snider, art director, for the beautiful cover design, and to Phil Mazzone for the overall classy look of the book. Thank you to managing editor Amelie Littell, and to Cheryl Mamaril, production manager. To photographer Chris Vaccaro, food stylist Cinzia Salvato, and food stylist assistant Becky Soares for the beautifully executed food shots. To Paul Lally, executive producer of *Ciao Italia,* my deepest respect; you are a rare dynamo who wears so many hats and who cares as deeply as I do about bringing home cooking back to the table. And to the hardworking friends at NETA who distribute our series, especially Gayle Loeber, Mary Ann Freeman, and Bob Petts. To my loyal agent, Michael Jones, for his wisdom and advice; to the kitchen support staff of *Ciao Italia,* Donna Petti Soares, head culinary supervisor, and culinary assistants and jacks of all trades Ruth Moore and Jennifer Chase Esposito, and all those behind the scenes, technical and otherwise, who make my work so much fun. To the national underwriters of the television series, Colavita USA, John Profaci, and the entire Profaci family, and to Jennifer Lionti, our liaison at Colavita USA. To Winebow Imports, especially Leonardo LoCascio, Helen Gallo Bryan, and Kristin Milles. Thank you to Venda Ravioli, Alan Costantino, and to *Italy Italy Magazine* and Stephania Nicotra for facilitating our stay in Italy, and also to Dave Anderson of King Arthur Flour. Many thanks to Dr. A. Ken Ciongoli, chairman of the National Italian American Foundation for all his help in getting us to Italy. To Rhode Island Public television, acting president David Piccerelli, director Jim Garret, and the entire Rhode Island public television crew who do such a fabulous job. To Nancy Radke, director for the Consorzio del Formaggio Parmigiano-Reggiano, for being a kind and generous friend, and for writing the foreword to this book. *Mille grazie* to friends in Italy who made our film journey to document authentic foods of the south so exciting, especially the Duke and Duchess of Fragnito Monforte, David and Patsy Montalto, and to the family of Esposito cousins in Benevento, whose home we invaded to film a charming episode with cousin Anna Esposito. In Molise, special thanks to superb winemakers Luigi and Alessio DiMajo Norante in Campomarino and *grazie* to winemaker Silvia Imparato in Montevetrano, and her sister, Anna Imparato, who runs the La Vecchia Quercia cooking school. And in Campobasso, thanks to Signor Carlo Fusco, Bette Gragnano, and Teresa D'Alessio, for their help in coordinating the Colavita pasta segment. To Rosella Genzale, chef of Filiberto Ristorante in Mirabella Eclano for allowing our crew to film a segment for *Ciao Italia*. Also thanks to chefs Mimmo and Ernesto of La Piana del Mulini Ristorazione in Colle d'Anchise for showcasing typical Molisana foods. To Cindy Jones, videographer, and Jeff Spence, sound recorder, two of the best I have ever worked with, and huge thanks to Donna Petti Soares, logistics manager and timekeeper, and one of the best friends I could ever wish for. To Nancy Starziano of Eastside Market in Providence, Rhode Island, and Olgo Russo of Russo's in Watertown, Massachusetts, who supplied us with all the ingredients for the shows, and to Panera Bread and Tonya Harms for feeding our crew with their delicious breads and baked goods. *Mille grazie tutti e un'abbraccione.*

Foreword

There are three secrets to authentic Italian cooking: use only absolutely fresh, flavorful ingredients; cook them quickly to preserve all their vibrant flavors and aromas; and serve them up to family and friends with love and flare. In this collection of splendid thirty-minute recipes, Mary Ann Esposito shows you how to make this true Italian culinary wisdom work for you.

I got my first taste of Italian cooking as a young American living in Rome more than twenty-five years ago. The Italian women in my apartment building, all grandmothers, thought I was much too young to be living so far from home and took me under their wings. Each day at eleven in the morning I would visit one of them, have some espresso (corrected with a touch of brandy), practice my fledgling Italian, and watch them put together a splendid three-course midday meal in a flash. The next day I'd run to the market, buy all the ingredients, and re-create the same fabulous, colorful, and quick meal that I had watched them prepare the day before. To my amazement and my husband's delight, I had turned into a respectable overnight Italian cook.

Now with Mary Ann Esposito by your side you can do the same thing. *Ciao Italia Pronto!* is a perfect guide, the fruit of Mary Ann's own rich culinary journey spent cooking joyfully every busy day of her life. First she instructs you on the basics. Build and maintain a pantry (dry and refrigerated) filled with Italian staples like olive oil, anchovies, capers, oil-packed tuna, herbs, pasta, cheeses, cured meats, and a couple of freezer items. These essentials will become your launching pad for preparing her recipes and for creatively branching out on your own.

Her tips for organization and shopping are smart and practical. I am in the process of building up my Italian pantry in my new second home, and following Mary Ann's advice has been fun. First I skimmed *Ciao Italia Pronto!* and discovered a wonderful section of suggested menus in the back of the book. I picked the easy company dinner, made my list (doubling up on the staples), and headed to the store. Without much work we enjoyed a marvelous feast that started with tasty and warm Little Ciabatta Toasts with Ricotta and Salami, then featured crisply coated Skillet Breaded Pork Chops with Rosemary that I served on a bed of intense pan-sautéed Cherry Tomatoes with Leeks and Thyme, and concluded with the easiest dessert in the world, Dried Figs in Red Wine. The best part is that I now have all the necessary staples on hand to make Mary Ann's menu again or to use in something else.

Beyond her organizational tips you will find that Mary Ann's recipes are the real treasure. They bring you the wonderful unfussy and flavorful fare that Italians love to eat every day of the week. This is the food my family and I love to eat as well, and we're not even Italian! That's because this is the food of life and good health. In these pages you will find some of the most delicious examples of healthy Italian cooking based on the use of monounsaturated olive oil, pasta made from durum wheat (which has finally been reinstated in the USDA food pyramid as the superior carbohydrate it has always been), abundant fresh vegetables and fruits, cured meats like prosciutto di Parma, and aged cheeses like Parmigiano-Reggiano and pecorino romano that come from carefully controlled districts in Italy and bear guarantees of naturalness and artisan craftsmanship.

You may have purchased this book for its quick recipes, but Mary Ann is also giving you the tools to prepare better-tasting, healthier food. Make yourself the

Pastina and Egg Soup with Spinach one night for a quick dinner or serve your friends some Whole Wheat Fettuccine with Mushrooms and Walnuts or get the kids hooked on Fried Fish Fillets with Almond and Parmesan Cheese Coating and Green Beans in Tomato Sauce and you'll see what I mean. Soon you and everyone you love will be eating better and you never will become a slave to the kitchen.

This is Mary Ann's gift to you in *Ciao Italia Pronto!*

—Nancy R. Radke
Director
U.S. Information Office
Consorzio del Formaggio Parmigiano-Reggiano

Introduction

Creating the concept for this book has been a unique experience because the intent was to focus on the preparation of uncomplicated recipes that could be on the table in short order. It is no secret that today's overbusy lifestyle impacts the way we think about and prepare food at home. We want to eat healthfully, but we don't want to spend hours in the kitchen at the end of the day. And the good news is that we don't have to.

Pronto means "ready" in Italian, but we associate it with being quick, and this book, a companion to the television series *Ciao Italia,* is designed to get you organized and in and out of the kitchen effortlessly without compromising the authenticity and taste of Italian food. It is filled with more than eighty easy-to-prepare dishes, many inspired from my travels in Italy over the years, and from guest chefs who have appeared in show segments of *Ciao Italia.*

These recipes take thirty minutes or less to prepare and/or cook and are streamlined to take into account busy schedules. I offer them to you with practical advice and many shortcuts that will have you happily sitting down at the table with time to relax and enjoy your efforts.

Believe it or not, I cook every night, and when I am out of town teaching others about the merits of home cooking, I leave ready-made meals in the freezer for my family. So I know what saving time means to busy people. I am busy, too.

The key to having good food on the table fast without a hassle is simple. Be prepared. How?

- **First**, have a basic pantry stocked with staple items such as olive oil, vinegar, wine, and pasta. See the suggested pantry items on page 5.
- **Second**, have a plan. That means never go into a supermarket without a shopping list. It is far better to have a written list than to wander willy-nilly through the aisles wondering what to buy. Get in the habit of taking stock of what you have in the refrigerator, freezer, and pantry. Once a month buy staple items such as flour, sugar, canned broths—things that have shelf life. Then fill in your weekly shopping with the fresh items that you will need. Designate a day—Wednesdays are often best—when most newspapers focus on food-circular features. Make a weekly menu plan based on it and what you and your family like to eat. Shop around features. For example, if turkey is on sale and your family loves it, buy it and turn it into a delicious Neapolitan-style version (page 90), or use it to add to low-sodium canned broth with some frozen vegetables and pastina or other soup pasta for a quick supper teamed with a fresh garden salad.
- **Third**, learn to multitask. For instance, if you are preparing vegetables for one meal, prepare extra for the next night as well. In my family, salads are a nightly must, but the one job that I dislike more than anything else (even cleaning squid) is cleaning lettuce. So when I do, I clean enough to get me through four or five days, saving me the tedium of having to do it every night.
- **Fourth**, cook so as to get several meals for your effort. It is just as easy to make two Lazy Lasagnes (page 48) and freeze one for later as it is to go through the motions for making one.
- **Fifth**, cook with in-season fruits and vegetables; this is healthier for you and lends variety to meals. And take advantage of fresh-frozen vegetables and

those ready-cut varieties in zip-lock bags found in the produce section. They save lots of cutting and dicing time.

- **Sixth**, maximize the use of your freezer and stock it with meals prepared ahead on the weekend.
- **Seventh**, never shop early in the week when many supermarkets are out of key items due to weekend shoppers; this will only frustrate you and necessitate another trip, causing loss of precious time. And if you have to shop on the weekend or your day off, go early.
- **Eighth**, think creatively. Here is an example: If you buy one of those supermarket rotisserie-roasted chickens, you can get several meals out of it. Part of it can be cut up into small pieces and added to low-sodium canned broth with a few vegetables or fresh spinach for a nourishing and respectable soup. Part of it can be made into chicken salad, or how about a quick chicken pie? And those chicken bones—don't throw them away: throw them into a pot, cover them with water, add a carrot or two, celery tops, an onion, and some spices and simmer to get a flavorful stock.
- **Ninth**, revisit the word *leftovers*. You will be surprised at what you can do by just using your imagination and the leftovers in your refrigerator. How do you think casseroles arrived in the kitchen? Look at some of the surprising things you can make with leftovers on page 102.
- **Tenth**, get everyone in your household involved, including children. This is key to having the next generation be able to identify good food choices and acquire the skills to cook sensibly. Remember, cooking is more than satisfying hunger; it can be a great connector, a healer, a confidence builder, and just plain fun. Once you start, you will be inspired to do more.

Like anything else in life, preparation is everything. Getting good food on the table can take only minutes, but the bonds and memories that are forged can last a lifetime. Let this book be a guide that shows you how easy it can be to have good food on the table *pronto*!

Pronto Pantry

Nothing fascinated me more as a child than my Sicilian grandmother's walk-in pantry. To this day I can still vividly recall the smells of garlic, cheese, olive oil, wine, and onions lining the shelves. My grandmother's pantry was large, and everything she needed for her cooking was right at hand. She never wondered what there was for supper because she knew what was in that pantry.

I have a large walk-in pantry, too, with an extra refrigerator and freezer, partly because I need it for my work as a chef and partly because it is my food security blanket. I stock it with items I use all the time, from spices to grains to olive oils, tuna, anchovies, wine, pasta, and many other things. I believe in pantries, large or small, to help the cook save time. For me it is the most important place in the kitchen because that is where you will find the foundation for everyday meals. A pantry is an open invitation to cook, to be creative. A pantry keeps you organized, lets you see what your cooking preferences are, helps you plan ahead, and can challenge you. Open the cupboard or pantry door and inspiration stands before you. Even if your kitchen is small, there should be some space that is reserved for basic staples, things that are common ingredients for lots of your favorite dishes. And a pantry is not just where you store your cereal; think of your refrigerator and your freezer as extensions of the pantry.

Here is a suggested list of ingredients found in the recipes in this book. Some belong on a pantry shelf, others on your refrigerator shelf, and still others on your freezer shelf. If you have them, or at least some of them, you will never be in that unsettled quandary about what to cook for dinner. A pantry is food in the bank, so to speak, that you can draw from anytime. So take stock in your pantry items, the building blocks of fast but good food.

Dry Staples

Almonds. Whole roasted, unsalted. Once opened, keep refrigerated.

Anchovies in olive oil.

Anise extract. Be sure it is pure extract, meaning 35 percent alcohol.

Basil. Very perishable. Keep it with stems, not leaves, in water in a container on your counter; it will wilt under refrigerator conditions. Freeze the leaves in small plastic bags for use in soups, sauces, and stews but not for salad, as the leaves will be limp when defrosted. Throw them frozen into whatever you are making.

Bay leaves. Turkish are most flavorful; find them in the spice aisle.

Bouillon cubes. Vegetable, chicken, beef.

Broths, canned low-sodium. Chicken, beef, and vegetable.

Capers in salt or brine.

Celery salt. Gives great flavor to soups and stews.

Chickpeas, canned.

Chocolate, bittersweet. Good brands are Lindt and Callebaut.

Cinnamon, ground.

Clam juice, bottled.

Cloves, ground.

Cornmeal. Stone ground is best but all-purpose will do, or use the already prepared polenta sold in a cylinder shape; just cut and sauté or heat and use as directed in recipes.

Fennel seeds. Great in pork dishes.

Flour, unbleached all-purpose. King Arthur flour is used in recipes in this book.

Fruits, dried. Apricots, figs.

Garlic. Keep it in a garlic keeper or mesh bag in a cool, dark spot.

Honey.

Jelly, apple. Works well when melted and used as a glaze for tarts.

Marmalade, orange.

Mustard, Dijon. Use in marinades.

Nutmeg, ground.

Olive oil, extra-virgin. Think about your palate; do you like fruity-tasting olive oils? Then go for the ones from the south, from Umbria, Puglia, Molise, or Sicily. If you prefer light-tasting oil, go for those from Tuscany or Liguria.

Olive oil spray. Colavita is a good brand.

Olives, oil-cured black jarred.

Onions. Keep in a dark, cool place.

Oregano, dried. The only herb to ever use dried.

Panko bread crumbs. These Japanese crumbs are best for coating and frying since they are big and flaky. Or use good day-old bread; dry it out in a 250°F. oven until it is hard, then whirl it in a food processor to make fine crumbs, or put the bread in a bag and use a rolling pin to pulverize it.

Pasta. The following types should be kept on hand: **ditalini** (a small pasta used for soups), **fettuccine** (ribbonlike noodles), **fusilli** (corkscrew pasta), **no-boil lasagna** (I prefer Del Verde), **orzo** and **pastina** (tiny soup pasta), **spaghetti**, and **vermicelli** (thin pasta). Colavita, Del Verde, Barilla, and La Molisana are good brands.

Pepper, coarse black. Buy it already ground or use a pepper mill and grind whole peppercorns.

Potatoes, all-purpose white (for soups), **russet** (for baking), **Yukon Gold** (for mashing), and **red-skin** (for oven roasting) are my favorites. Keep in a dark area but not in a tightly closed bag; otherwise they will sprout.

Red pepper flakes, hot.

Rice. Arborio is a short-grain starchy rice used for making risotto; **long-grain rice** is used for soups and stuffings.

Salt. Use fine and coarse **sea salt.**

Sugar.

Tomatoes, canned plum. Peeled and crushed.

Tuna in olive oil, canned.

Vanilla beans. The seed of an orchid plant; find it in the baking section.

Vanilla extract, 35 percent alcohol. Do not use Mexican vanilla; use Madagascar. Good brands are Nielsen-Massey and Rodelle.

Vinegar, balsamic. Authentic *tradizionale* will cost over $75; use it sparingly as a condiment for meat, cheese, and dessert. Use a grocery store commercial type (which is really wine vinegar with a little balsamic thrown in) for everyday salads and marinades.

Vinegar, red wine.

Wines, red and white: Do not use cooking wines; they contain more sulfites and salt than regular wines and are more expensive. Buy inexpensive reds and whites such as Corvo, Folinari, and Regaleali. My rule: any wine you drink you can cook with. Store opened bottles in the refrigerator and invest in a vacuum seal pump, which you can find in wine stores.

Yeast, dried. If you make a lot of yeast dough, buy yeast in bulk and keep it in the refrigerator; otherwise buy the small packets. Store in a dry spot.

Refrigerator Pantry Basics

Butter, unsalted. Unsalted is fresher than salted.

Carrots. Baby carrots cook faster; find various cuts in the produce section from coins to julienne.

Celery. Use the leaves in soups and egg salad; wrap celery in paper towels to keep it crisp under refrigeration.

Cheeses:

Caciocavallo is a cow's milk cheese that is good for eating, grating, and melting.

Gorgonzola dolce, which is very perishable, is a versatile cheese with many uses, from sauce to a great dessert with ripe pears and a few walnuts. **Gorgonzola forte** is aged gorgonzola, and it has a stronger taste.

Mascarpone cheese is a full-fat soft cream cheese used in desserts like tiramisù and in cream sauces.

Fior di latte mozzarella cheese (a cow's milk cheese that is especially good for melting) is indispensable. You may also be able to find **mozzarella di bufala,** which is imported from Italy and has a delicate texture and taste and makes a wonderful *caprese* salad.

Parmigiano-Reggiano and **pecorino** cheeses are primarily used for grating, but are also eaten in small chunks or chips. Wedges of parmesan and pecorino will keep a long time in the warmest part of your fridge if they are wrapped in damp cheesecloth, then plastic wrap, and lastly in foil. Bring them to room temperature before eating.

Provolone cheese is great in sandwiches and on an antipasto platter.

Ricotta cheese is best if freshly made, but pasteurized will do.

Scamorza cheese is a smoked or unsmoked cow's milk cheese.

Eggs, large. Keep in their carton, not on the refrigerator door shelf.

Egg Beaters. For when you are really in a hurry.

Fennel, fresh. Licorice-tasting Italian celery in the salad department.

Ham.

Lemons. Bring to room temperature before using to extract more juice.

Lettuces. Romaine, arugula, escarole, radicchio.

Nuts. Pine nuts, walnuts. Toast them first in a dry nonstick sauté pan until lightly browned to really bring out their flavor.

Oranges. Bring to room temperature before using.

Pancetta. Italian unsmoked bacon. Can substitute for ham in recipes.

Parsley. Flat leaf, not curly, which has no flavor.

Radicchio. A chicory with a slightly bitter taste used for grilling and salads; find it in the produce section.

Rosemary. Small packages are available in the produce department. Keep a plant at home in a cool spot. It does not like to be near a heat source.

Sopressata. Or other hard salami.

Thyme. See note for rosemary.

Freezer Pantry Basics

Artichoke hearts. Great in pasta dishes, frittata, or on pizza dough.

Breads, artisanal. Whole grain and sourdough types. If you don't need to use a whole loaf, slice it and freeze slices in a zip-lock bag; that will make defrosting easy.

Broccoli, chopped.

Peas.

Pizza dough, store-bought. Not as good as homemade but good enough when you are pressed for time.

Puff pastry.

Shrimp, cooked and cleaned.

Spinach, chopped.

Tomato sauce, prepared. Made from scratch in batches and frozen.

Vegetables, mixed.

Pronto Antipasti

Datteri con Parmigiano-Reggiano e Noci (Dates Stuffed with Parmesan and Nuts)

Crostini di Ciabatta con Ricotta e Sopressata (Little Ciabatta Toasts with Ricotta and Salami)

Involtini di Zucchine e Zucca (Zucchini and Summer Squash Bundles)

Mozzarella in Carrozza (Fried Mozzarella Sandwiches)

Scapece (Marinated Fish)

Spiedini di Mozzarella con Prosciutto e Pomodoro (Mozzarella, Prosciutto, and Tomato Skewers)

Torta di Cozze e Gamberi (Mussel and Shrimp Tart)

Tortine di Formaggio (Little Cheese Tarts)

Antipasto is like the prelude to a good orchestral score. It is meant to get you in the mood and builds the anticipation of a great meal with small offerings of a variety of foods that lead to a crescendo of more elaborate things to follow. It usually means foods that are served at room temperature, and can be something as simple as oil-cured olives, pickled zucchini and sweet peppers, marinated artichokes, or cured meats such as prosciutto or salami. And many of you, I am sure, are familiar with the classic prosciutto with melon or figs.

Occasionally I make a meal just out of antipasto, especially in warm weather months when it is best to keep the kitchen cool. The beauty of antipasto is that it can be assembled ahead of time. For a party, why not make all the recipes in this chapter and let guests help themselves to variety and fun.

Datteri con Parmigiano-Reggiano e Noci
Dates Stuffed with Parmesan and Nuts

I love this antipasto (or even dessert) idea from Nancy Radke, the director for the Consorzio del Formaggio Parmigiano-Reggiano. Plump Medjool dates stuffed with chips of Parmesan cheese and pecan halves are ready in minutes and there is no cooking! Plan on serving two per person as these are rich and addictive.

Serves 12

---

24 whole dates

24 small chips of Parmigiano-Reggiano cheese at room temperature

24 pecan halves

With a small knife make a slit down the center of each date. Remove and discard the pit. Stuff the cavity with 1 chip of the cheese and 1 pecan half.

Arrange the dates on a tray and serve with a glass of champagne or Italian dessert wine.

Crostini di Ciabatta con Ricotta e Sopressata
Little Ciabatta Toasts with Ricotta and Salami

Crostini (little toasts) are always popular nibbles for an antipasto. But simple as these are to put together, the results depend entirely on good, dense bread, the kind in which the crust almost cuts the roof of your mouth. I use that analogy because soggy, spongy bread will simply not work for *crostini*, since the bread is toasted and then rubbed with a garlic clove. The bread must be sturdy enough to act as a grater when the garlic is rubbed over it. *Ciabatta* bread, a flat bread, is sturdy and readily available. It holds a spread of seasoned creamy ricotta cheese sprinkled with zippy and sassy *sopressata*, a dried pork salami.

Serves 8

---

1 cup fresh ricotta cheese

¼ cup grated pecorino cheese

2 tablespoons minced fresh basil

Salt to taste

Coarse black pepper to taste

8 slices ciabatta bread, cut ½ inch thick

Olive oil spray

1 large garlic clove, peeled

⅔ cup diced sopressata

Preheat the oven to 350°F.

Mix the cheeses, basil, salt, and pepper together in a small bowl. Set aside.

Place the bread slices on a baking sheet and bake them until lightly brown or toasted.

Transfer the slices to a cutting board and rub the garlic clove several times across the surface of each one. Spray each slice with olive oil.

Spread some of the ricotta mixture over each slice. Place the slices on a serving dish. Sprinkle some of the sopressata over each one. Serve.

Involtini di Zucchine e Zucca
Zucchini and Summer Squash Bundles

No zucchini? Unthinkable in an Italian kitchen. That is why this beloved vegetable is so open to interpretation. Sauté it, pickle it, boil it, grill it, and you have some of the classic preparations. But here is a technique that is just a little on the edge of *cucina alta* (gourmet cooking), a neat bundle of grilled zucchini and summer squash sandwiched together with a delicate ricotta cheese, lemon, and walnut filling. Sometimes the unexpected can be a refreshing change from the ordinary. Serve this as an antipasto, a lunch with a side of salad greens, or a light supper.

Saving time: Make and refrigerate the filling up to 2 days ahead.

Serves 4

---

1 cup ricotta cheese, well drained

Zest of 1 large lemon

1 tablespoon minced flat-leaf parsley

1 teaspoon minced fresh thyme

¼ teaspoon salt

Coarse black pepper to taste

⅓ cup finely chopped walnuts

2 medium zucchini at least 8 inches long

2 medium yellow summer squash at least 8 inches long

Olive oil spray

⅓ cup extra-virgin olive oil

Beat the ricotta cheese with a hand mixer until light and fluffy. Stir in the lemon zest, parsley, thyme, salt, pepper, and walnuts and set aside.

Preheat an indoor or outdoor grill.

Trim the zucchini and squash ends. Slice each into 4 lengthwise strips ¼ inch thick and place them on a baking sheet. Spray the slices with the olive oil on both sides and place them in a single layer on the grill. Grill on both sides until the strips are soft but not mushy. Transfer them to the baking sheet to cool.

Top a summer squash strip with a zucchini strip; trim the ends if necessary to make them even. Spread a thin layer of the ricotta cheese mixture on top of the zucchini strip. Start at one end and roll the strips up together like a jelly roll. Make 7 more. Place 2 rolls on each of 4 plates.

Warm the olive oil in a small saucepan and pour a little over each plate. Serve.

Note: *If you do not have a grill, place the strips on a baking sheet, lightly sprayed with oil, and bake them in a preheated 350°F. oven for 5 to 8 minutes or until they soften. Then proceed with the recipe.*

Mozzarella in Carrozza
Fried Mozzarella Sandwiches

Mozzarella in carrozza translates to the ultimate fried or grilled cheese sandwich and is a specialty of the region of Campania, where creamy mozzarella balls are made from buffalo milk. *Mozzarella di bufala* is best consumed *di giornata*, on the day it is made. Even though it is available here, the taste is not exactly the same, due to transportation. This is the perfect antipasto, and perfection is achieved by using the best buffalo mozzarella cheese and coarse bread. (Cow's milk mozzarella, known as *fior di latte*, is readily available and can be substituted for buffalo mozzarella.)

Serves 4

2 (8-ounce) balls buffalo mozzarella, or fior di latte cheese,
   cut into 8 slices
8 bread slices, cut ½ inch thick
4 large eggs
Pinch of salt
2 cups milk
½ cup canola or sunflower oil

Place 2 slices of mozzarella between each of 2 slices of bread to make 4 sandwiches. Set aside.

Lightly beat the eggs, salt, and milk with a fork or a whisk in a wide bowl.

Heat 2 tablespoons of the oil in a nonstick skillet large enough to hold at least 2 sandwiches.

Coat the sandwiches in the egg batter and fry them in batches on both sides in the oil until they are golden brown and the cheese begins to melt. Add additional oil as necessary if the pan becomes dry.

Serve hot, cut into quarters, as part of an antipasto or individually as sandwiches.

Scapece
Marinated Fish

The Spaniards may have introduced this marinated fish dish, *scapece* (from *escabèche*, meaning pickled, in Spanish), to Italy. The flavors develop over the course of several hours or overnight under refrigeration. *Scapece* is best served with chunky wedges of ripe tomatoes and lemons. Have slices of good crusty bread to mop up the tasty juices.

Serves 4 to 6

⅔ cup extra-virgin olive oil

2 garlic cloves, finely minced

⅓ cup red wine vinegar

⅓ cup minced fresh mint leaves

Salt and black pepper to taste

½ cup flour

1 pound sole or flounder, cut into 4-inch pieces

⅓ cup canola oil

1 cup toasted bread crumbs

Combine the olive oil, garlic, vinegar, mint leaves, and salt and pepper in a bowl and set aside. Have ready a 9 × 12-inch baking dish or similar dish. Set aside.

Pour the flour into a paper or plastic bag. Place the fish pieces in the bag and shake to coat them evenly. Fry the pieces quickly, a few at a time, on both sides in the canola oil until they begin to brown. Gently remove the pieces with a slotted metal spatula and transfer them to brown paper to drain. Place a single layer of fish in the dish and then sprinkle some of the crumbs over the top. Continue making layers of fish and bread crumbs, ending with the bread crumbs. Pour the marinade over the top. Cover the dish and marinate in the refrigerator overnight. Allow the dish to come to room temperature before serving.

Spiedini di Mozzarella con Prosciutto e Pomodoro
Mozzarella, Prosciutto, and Tomato Skewers

It has become all the rage in Italy to offer an array of antipasti for a gathering of friends instead of a traditional sit-down meal. Italian food shops known as *alimentari* sell exquisitely prepared ones that reflect the local products. A colorful and unusual favorite are *bocconcini*, tiny balls of mozzarella cheese wrapped in prosciutto that are skewered with bread cubes and cherry tomatoes. This chic presentation comes from chef Alberto Lopez of Constantino's restaurant in Providence, Rhode Island. Double or triple the recipe to serve more guests.

Serves 8

---

16 wooden skewers
16 bocconcini (small mozzarella balls)
8 thin slices prosciutto di Parma, cut in half width-wise
16 grape or cherry tomatoes
16 (1-inch) bread cubes
Extra-virgin olive oil
8 shaved strips Parmigiano-Reggiano cheese
6 basil leaves, cut into thin strips

Wrap each mozzarella ball in a half-slice of the prosciutto. Thread each skewer with a mozzarella ball, tomato, and bread cube. Repeat the sequence.

Arrange the skewers on a platter. Drizzle the oil over the skewers and sprinkle the cheese and basil over them.

Torta di Cozze e Gamberi
Mussel and Shrimp Tart

Neapolitans know what they like, and they like *cozze* (mussels) a lot. Tossed with pasta, eaten with bread in a mussel soup (*zuppa di cozze*), or served as a delicate tart, mussels are as close to a Neapolitan's heart as one can get. Inspiration for this mussel and shrimp combination, blanketed in a velvety egg and cream custard, comes from the many times I have enjoyed mussels in Naples. Prepared puff pastry makes this tart fun to prepare and elegant enough to serve as a party antipasto or main entrée.

Serves 6 to 8

1 sheet commercially prepared puff pastry, thawed in the refrigerator
48 mussels, washed and debearded
½ cup white wine
1 cup cooked shrimp (18 to 20)
1 teaspoon salt
Coarse black pepper to taste
¼ cup minced flat-leaf parsley
2 eggs
⅔ cup heavy cream
¼ cup finely minced red onion
½ cup diced sweet red pepper

Preheat the oven to 425°F.

Roll the pastry dough out to fit a 9-inch tart pan with a removable bottom. Line the bottom and sides. Cut off any excess dough.

Place a sheet of aluminum foil over the dough and scatter a handful of dried beans or rice over it. This will help to prevent the pastry dough from puffing up while it is baking.

Bake the tart shell for 5 to 7 minutes or just until it begins to brown. Remove from the oven. Remove the aluminum foil with the beans or rice and discard them. Cool the tart shell while you prepare the filling.

Lower the oven temperature to 375°F.

Put the mussels in a sauté pan. Add the wine, cover the pan, and steam the mussels until they open. Discard any mussels that do not open. Remove the mussels from their shells and set them aside. Strain and reserve the mussel liquid.

Toss the mussels and shrimp together in a small bowl with the salt, pepper, and parsley. Transfer the mixture to the cooled tart shell. Place the tart shell on a rimmed baking sheet to catch any drips.

In a small bowl whisk together the eggs, 2 tablespoons of the reserved mussel juice, the cream, onion, and red pepper. Pour evenly over the mussel and shrimp mixture.

Bake the tart until set, about 25 to 30 minutes. Cool slightly. Cut into wedges.

Tortine di Formaggio
Little Cheese Tarts

Pasta sfoglia means puff pastry, those magical thin layers of dough that get their great flakiness from loads of butter. Anyone who has ever made it knows that it takes time. But a respectable alternative is to use good commercially prepared puff pastry for these savory cheese *tortine*, little cheese tarts.

Saving time: Roll and line the tart shells with the pastry and refrigerate them, unfilled, for up to 2 days. Or line and freeze them individually wrapped. When ready to bake, do not defrost them, simply fill and bake.

Serves 4 to 6

---

1 sheet commercially prepared puff pastry, thawed in the refrigerator

4 to 6 3½ × ¾-inch tart shells with removable bottoms

1 cup diced prosciutto

1 cup grated Parmigiano-Reggiano cheese

4 large eggs, lightly beaten

2 tablespoons minced flat-leaf parsley

2 cups half-and-half

½ teaspoon salt

Grated nutmeg to taste

Preheat oven to 425°F.

Roll the pastry on a lightly floured board to a 14 × 14-inch square. Cut out four to six 5-inch circles. Line each tart shell with 1 circle of pastry dough. Use scraps to line more shells if enough dough is left.

Divide and sprinkle the prosciutto on the bottom of each tart shell. Divide and sprinkle the cheese over the prosciutto.

In a bowl whisk the eggs, parsley, half-and-half, salt, and nutmeg together. Divide and pour the mixture over the tart shells. Place the tart shells on a rimmed baking sheet to catch any drips.

Bake for 10 to 15 minutes or just until the filling sets. Remove the baking sheet from the oven. Transfer the tarts to a cooling rack.

When cool enough to handle, remove the bottoms of the tart shells. Place the tarts on individual dishes and serve with red beet and orange salad.

Pronto Soups

Minestra di Zucchine con Cacio e Uove (Zucchini Soup with Cheese and Eggs)

Zuppa di Pastina all' Uova e Spinaci (Pastina and Egg Soup with Spinach)

Zuppa di Pollo alla Tomasino (Tomie's from Scratch Chicken Soup)

Zuppa di Polpettine (Meatball Soup)

Zuppa di Pollo Fine Settimana (Weekend Chicken Soup)

A good soup is judged on the quality of the ingredients used and the care taken to make it. That doesn't mean you must spend hours in the kitchen. Look over the soups in this chapter. There are three quick ones, ready in less than half an hour, and two I call "weekend soups" that are easy to put together but require a little more cooking time. Once made, they can carry you through the week when you are rushed. Team these soups with a salad and some fresh fruit, and dinner is effortless and satisfying. If you have followed my advice on stocking the Pronto Pantry, you have everything you need for making them.

Minestra di Zucchine con Cacio e Uove
Zucchini Soup with Cheese and Eggs

This old-fashioned soup with zucchini, cheese, and eggs is served over slices of stale bread. Use small-size zucchini; they are more tender and will cook faster.

Serves 4 to 6

2 tablespoons extra-virgin olive oil

5 small zucchini, ends trimmed, washed and diced

4 cups hot chicken broth or water

Salt and pepper to taste

2 eggs

⅓ cup grated pecorino or Parmigiano-Reggiano cheese

Small bunch of basil leaves, torn into small pieces

Heat the olive oil in a soup pot and cook the zucchini until lightly browned. Pour in the broth or water. Season with salt and pepper and cook for 10 minutes.

Whisk together the eggs and the cheese in a bowl and pour it into the soup. Stir well. Stir in the basil. Serve the soup as is or ladled over fried bread slices.

Zuppa di Pastina all' Uova e Spinaci
Pastina and Egg Soup with Spinach

Pastina, those tiny "beads" of hard semolina pasta, always have a place in chicken soup, and children especially seem to love scooping them up. This version takes minutes to prepare with canned low-sodium chicken or vegetable broth. But if you want to make it using homemade broth, see the easy recipe on page 32 for making broth ahead and freezing it for future use. This recipe can easily be cut in half.

🕐 **Saving time:** Cleaned, packaged spinach is in the produce section all ready to use.

Serves 8

---

2 quarts prepared low-sodium chicken or vegetable broth

1 cup pastina

4 cups washed spinach leaves, torn into small pieces, or 2 packages frozen spinach, defrosted and well drained

4 eggs

1 cup grated Parmigiano-Reggiano cheese

Bring the broth to a boil in a soup pot, stir in the pastina, cover the pot, and cook for 5 minutes over medium high heat. Lower the heat to medium, stir in the fresh or frozen and defrosted spinach, and cook for 1 minute.

Whisk the eggs and cheese together in a soup tureen or deep bowl.

Slowly ladle the hot soup into the soup tureen; stir the soup as you ladle. The heat will cook the egg. Serve immediately.

Zuppa di Pollo alla Tomasino
Tomie's from Scratch Chicken Soup

Tomie dePaola, the noted children's illustrator and author, is a fine cook and crazy about his Italian heritage. He appears often on segments of *Ciao Italia* with classic recipes from southern Italy. Here is his chicken soup made from scratch. Kept on hand in the freezer, it can serve you well in the kitchen in a multitude of ways, from using it as a savory broth, or with tiny meatballs or vegetables, as a basis making sauce.

Makes about 2 quarts

2 to 5 whole cloves

1 onion, unpeeled

2 flat-leaf parsley sprigs

1 tarragon sprig

1 thyme sprig

1 bay leaf

10 to 12 whole black peppercorns

2 pounds assorted chicken parts for soup, including wings and backs

2 celery ribs with leaves, rinsed and cut into chunks

3 carrots, scrubbed and cut into large chunks

1 teaspoon salt

Use the cloves to stud the onion. Put the onion in a soup pot. Tie the parsley, tarragon, and thyme together with kitchen string and add it to the pot. Wrap the bay leaf and peppercorns in a small piece of cheesecloth and tie with kitchen string to make a bouquet garni. Add it to the pot.

Rinse the chicken pieces and add them to the pot along with the celery and carrots.

Cover the ingredients with cold water and add the salt. Bring to a rolling boil and skim the foam and scum from the surface as it rises. Let the ingredients boil for several minutes, then lower the heat and simmer for several hours. Check to skim more foam as it rises and add more water, if necessary, to keep the ingredients submerged.

Line a colander with damp cheesecloth. Strain the stock, pressing down on the solids. Discard the solids.

Chill the stock, covered, in the refrigerator. The fat will rise to the top and solidify. It will be easy to remove by scraping the top with a spoon.

Serve the stock as a clear soup, or with added vegetables or noodles, or freeze it for future use.

Zuppa di Polpettine
Meatball Soup

Meatball soup is one of my choices for weekend cooking. I make enough so that it can also make an appearance on the table midweek served with Fried Mozzarella Sandwiches (page 20).

Saving time: Keeping a container of grated cheese in the refrigerator eliminates a step in this recipe.

Serves 6 to 8

---

2 bread slices, crusts removed

⅓ cup milk or ricotta cheese

¼ cup grated Parmigiano-Reggiano or pecorino cheese

1 tablespoon minced flat-leaf parsley

1 tablespoon grated lemon zest

Salt to taste

Coarse black pepper to taste

¼ pound ground chuck

¼ pound ground pork

¼ pound ground veal

1 (2-pound) bag frozen ready-to-cook mixed vegetables

2 quarts low-fat canned chicken or beef broth

1 (28-ounce) can diced plum tomatoes

Tear the bread into bite-size pieces and place them in a bowl. Pour the milk over the bread or stir in the ricotta cheese. Let the mixture stand for 5 minutes. Stir in the grated cheese, parsley, lemon zest, salt, and pepper and mix well. Add the meats and mix with your hands to blend the ingredients well.

Preheat the oven to 350°F.

Have a bowl of water handy to keep your hands wet while making the meatballs. Scoop up about 2 teaspoons of the mixture and roll it into a small ball with your hands. Place the meatballs on a lightly sprayed baking sheet. Continue making meatballs, spacing them on the baking sheet so that they're not touching. Bake the meatballs for about 12 minutes or until they begin to brown. Transfer them with a slotted spoon to a soup pot or crock pot. Stir in the vegetables and the broth. If the tomatoes are whole and not pre-diced, use a kitchen scissors to cut them into bits in the can and add them to the soup. Bring the mixture to a boil, lower the heat, and cook for 10 minutes.

Variation: Add 1 cup cooked small pasta like ditalini or elbows to the soup.

Zuppa di Pollo Fine Settimana
Weekend Chicken Soup

How about a really delicious, easy-to-prepare, chock-full of chicken soup for supper? With a ready-cooked rotisserie chicken from your local market, canned broth, and some frozen peas, this soup appears almost magically. And it is good enough for company.

Saving time: Buy the chicken several days ahead and debone it. Refrigerate the pieces until ready to put the soup together.

Serves 6 to 8

5½ cups homemade or canned low-sodium chicken broth

1 cup diced leeks or scallions

2 cups diced chicken from a 3-pound cooked rotisserie chicken

1 tablespoon celery seed

2 tablespoons minced flat-leaf parsley

Fine sea salt to taste

10 whole cherry tomatoes, stemmed and washed

1 cup frozen peas

2 tablespoons fresh lemon juice

Pour 1 cup of broth into a 2-quart soup pot; add the leeks or scallions, and bring the mixture to a simmer. Cook, covered, for 3 minutes or just until the leeks or scallions look wilted. Pour in the remaining broth and add the chicken, celery seed, parsley, and salt. Cover and cook 3 minutes more. Add the cherry tomatoes and peas and cook for 2 minutes. Stir in the lemon juice. Serve hot.

Variation: Add 1 can well-drained and rinsed chickpeas or 1 cup cooked ditalini pasta.

Pronto Pasta

Bucatini all' Amatriciana (Thick Spaghetti, Amatrice Style)

Fettuccine con Funghi e Noci (Whole Wheat Fettuccine with Mushrooms and Walnuts)

Fusilli con Ragù d'Agnello alla Molisana (Corkscrew Macaroni with Lamb Ragù, Molise Style)

Lasagne Pigre (Lazy Lasagne)

Frittata di Vermicelli Senza Uove (Vermicelli Pie Without Eggs)

Linguine al Limone e Panna (Linguine with Lemon and Cream)

Schiaffoni al Forno con Salsa di Asparagi (Oven-Baked Smacks with Asparagus Sauce)

Spaghetti con Tonno, Capperi e Limone (Spaghetti with Tuna, Capers, and Lemon)

Spaghetti Spezzati con Gamberi (Broken Spaghetti with Shrimp)

P asta is always considered pronto because not only can it be cooked in less than ten minutes but many sauces for it can be too, and there are so many ways to concoct a good pasta dish these days that there is really no excuse to resort to those so-called fancy frozen or canned ready-to-serve types.

Southern Italy is the home of dried pasta (*pasta secca*), in all forms, from short rigatoni with lines to *spagettoni* (long strings of spaghetti). In the past, southern Italians were referred to as *mangiamaccheroni*, or macaroni eaters, as it was and is a signature food in the diet. Macaroni was the all-inclusive word that meant pasta. When I was growing up, all pasta, whether made from semolina and water and store-bought, or fresh homemade with eggs and flour, was always called macaroni.

As we all know by now, pasta is a first course, but we treat it as a main course—and that is where pasta has gotten a bad name over the last few years and wound up on the food police's list of forbidden foods. Instead of serving small portions as is done in Italy, we dish up platter-size portions as individual servings. Restaurants are notorious for this practice.

When eaten in moderation and in small portions, pasta is and should be a part of any healthful diet. I am forever surprising people in my cooking seminars when I tell them that a pound of pasta serves eight people when they want it to serve two! And I know people who can eat a pound of pasta from the cooking pot just testing it for doneness! To keep things in perspective and in control, I have one of those handy spaghetti-measuring tools in my kitchen. It looks like a thick ruler with holes, and each hole holds a specific amount of pasta, so it is very useful when you want to gauge how much to cook for the number of people you are serving.

When is pasta cooked and when have you really gone over the edge? My rule is to fish out a piece as it is cooking and break it in half. Do you see white edges? This means you are looking at uncooked flour. Cook the pasta until you no longer see flour. It should remain al dente, firm but cooked through, and it should hold its original shape. There is nothing worse than overcooked, mushy pasta.

Here are some things to be aware of when cooking pasta. Remember to always use enough water, four to six quarts, and to use a large pasta pot with an insert, if possible. This makes it very easy to drain the pasta. Salt the water *after* it comes to a boil and before adding the pasta, using a generous tablespoon per pound, and never add oil to the cooking water, which will only make the pasta slick and prevent the sauce from adhering. If you use enough water to cook it in the first place, I guarantee that the pasta will not stick. Never rinse pasta after it is drained, which will only result in your washing away the necessary starch that helps the sauce stick. Follow these rules and perfectly cooked pasta will result every time.

Here are some of my favorite, unusual, and and quick-to-prepare pasta dishes. Make them as is or try them with some of the master sauces found on pages 61–71.

Bucatini all' Amatriciana
Thick Spaghetti, Amatrice Style

So many Italian dishes like *Bucatini all' Amatriciana* inherit their names from small regional places such as Amatrice, a town northeast of Rome. *Bucatini* looks like spaghetti, only thicker and with a hole. The sauce is not for timid taste buds. This is a dish filled with audacious flavors. Made with Italian bacon and hot red peppers, it is always served on August 16, the day after *ferragosto*, the beginning of the long and hot Italian summer holidays.

Serves 8

---

2 tablespoons extra-virgin olive oil

⅔ cup diced pancetta (Italian bacon)

1 medium onion, peeled and diced

1 teaspoon or more hot red pepper flakes or 1 small hot pepper, seeded and diced

4 cups canned crushed plum tomatoes

Salt to taste

Coarse black pepper to taste

1 pound bucatini

2 tablespoons unsalted butter

½ cup grated pecorino cheese

¼ cup reserved cooking water

Heat the olive oil in a sauté pan large enough to accommodate the bucatini after it is cooked. Stir in the pancetta and cook until it begins to crisp and crackle and turn a deep brown. Do not burn it. Stir in the onion and continue to cook until the onion softens. Stir in the red pepper and cook for 1 minute. Slowly pour in the tomatoes. Season with salt and pepper and simmer the sauce, covered, for 10 minutes. Keep the sauce warm while the bucatini is cooking.

Follow the directions for cooking pasta on pages 40–41. Drain the bucatini, reserving ¼ cup of the cooking water.

Combine the bucatini in a large bowl with the butter, cheese, and the reserved cooking water. Transfer the mixture to the sauté pan with the sauce. Reheat the mixture slowly until hot. Transfer the bucatini to a platter and serve immediately.

Note: *Originally pig's jowl and cheek, called* guanciale, *was used in place of bacon.*

Fettuccine con Funghi e Noci
Whole Wheat Fettuccine with Mushrooms and Walnuts

With its nutty flavor, whole wheat fettuccine plays off nicely in a sauce that is a mix of mushrooms, garlic, and toasted walnuts.

Saving time: Buy presliced, packaged fresh mushrooms and shelled, chopped walnut pieces.

Serves 8

---

2 garlic cloves, peeled
3 tablespoons fresh thyme leaves
½ cup walnut pieces
2 tablespoons extra-virgin olive oil
1 pound mixed mushrooms, including shiitake, cremini, and portobello
½ cup dry red wine
1 teaspoon balsamic vinegar
Fine sea salt to taste
Coarse black pepper to taste
1 pound whole wheat fettuccine
¼ cup reserved cooking water

Mince the garlic and thyme together and set aside.

Heat a large nonstick sauté pan over medium heat. Sprinkle the walnut pieces in the pan and, stirring with a wooden spoon, toast them for about 2 minutes. Transfer the nuts to a small dish.

Heat the oil in the same pan, stir in the garlic and thyme, and cook for 1 minute. Stir in the mushrooms and cook them until they exude their juices and begin to look dry. Raise the heat to high, stir in the wine and vinegar, and cook 1 minute. Lower the heat and stir in the salt and pepper. Keep the mixture warm.

Cook the fettuccine as directed on pages 40–41. Drain, reserving ¼ cup of the water. Add the fettuccine and water to the pan and cook, stirring over medium heat, until everything is hot. Transfer to a platter, sprinkle on the walnuts, and serve.

Fusilli con Ragù d'Agnello alla Molisana
Corkscrew Macaroni with Lamb Ragù, Molise Style

This is the typical lamb sauce for pasta dishes that make up the distinct cooking of the regions of Molise and Abruzzi. This sauce is perfect for *fusillioni*, the larger version of a twisted pasta more familiar to us as fusilli, which is readily available in your supermarket. The name *fusilli* comes from the knitting-needle-type implement used by hand long ago to form the dough into its twisted or corkscrew shape. It is ideal for trapping the sauce in its curves and grooves. If you want to give this sauce a lively kick, add a small diced hot red pepper.

Saving time: The sauce can be made ahead and frozen for up to 3 months. Double the ingredients to make 2 batches.

Serves 8

3 garlic cloves, peeled

2 tablespoons fresh rosemary needles

¼ cup extra-virgin olive oil

2 whole bay leaves

2 medium sweet red peppers, seeded, cut into thin strips, and diced

1 small hot red pepper, seeded and diced, or 1 teaspoon dried red pepper flakes or to taste (optional)

1 pound ground lamb

⅔ cup dry white wine

6 large plum tomatoes, seeded and chopped, juice reserved, or 1 (16-ounce) can

Salt to taste

Coarse black pepper to taste

1 pound fusilli

Grated pecorino cheese for sprinkling

Mince the garlic and rosemary together. Set aside.

Heat the olive oil in a 2-quart saucepan over medium heat and cook the garlic mixture along with the bay leaves until the garlic softens.

Stir in the peppers and hot pepper, if using, and cook for 2 minutes until the peppers soften. Stir in the lamb and brown it slowly, breaking it up with a spoon as it cooks. Raise the heat to medium-high, pour in the wine, and stir the ingredients with a wooden spoon until most of the wine evaporates.

Stir in the tomatoes and their juice, and the salt and pepper. Cover the saucepan, lower the heat to simmer, and cook for 25 to 30 minutes. At the end of the cooking, remove and discard the bay leaves.

Cook the fusilli according to the directions on pages 40–41. Drain the fusilli and add it to the saucepan. Stir to coat it well with the sauce. Transfer the mixture to a serving platter. Sprinkle the cheese over the top and serve.

Lasagne Pigre

Lazy Lasagne

Layered lasagne sheets filled with a slathering of ricotta cheese, spinach, and grated Parmesan cheese are baking, all nestled under a blanket of tomato sauce. And the nice thing is that making it takes only 10 minutes when you use no-boil lasagne sheets, tomato sauce made ahead, and have frozen vegetables on hand. In less than an hour, the hypnotic aroma of homemade lasagne brings everyone to the table. There are many brands of no-boil lasagne such as Del Verde, which can be found in grocery stores. This recipe was tested with Del Verde no-boil lasagne sheets, which come with their own 9-inch aluminum baking pans.

Saving time: the recipe makes two 9-inch-square pans; freeze one for later use.

Makes two 9-inch-square pans, enough for each to serve 4 to 6

---

2 (16-ounce) containers skim milk ricotta cheese, drained

2 large eggs or 4 egg whites

1 (10-ounce) package frozen spinach leaves, defrosted and squeezed dry

2 teaspoons salt

Coarse black pepper to taste

1½ cups grated Parmigiano-Reggiano cheese

4 cups prepared Tomato Sauce (page 69)

10 no-boil Del Verde lasagne sheets

Preheat the oven to 350°F.

In a bowl combine the ricotta cheese, eggs or egg whites, spinach, salt and pepper, and ½ cup of the grated cheese. Mix well and set aside.

Ladle ½ cup of the tomato sauce in each of 2 pans and spread it thinly. Place 1 lasagne sheet on top of the sauce and spread ½ cup of the ricotta cheese mixture over the top in each pan.

Sprinkle ¼ cup of the grated cheese over each pan. Add another lasagne sheet and repeat the process, making 3 layers of ricotta cheese and sauce. Divide and sprinkle the remaining grated cheese on top of the last layer. Top with the last lasagne sheet and spread on the remaining sauce. Cover each pan tightly with aluminum foil and place the pans on baking sheets to catch any drips.

Bake for 30 to 35 minutes. Allow to stand 5 minutes before cutting to allow the noodles to firm up. Cut into squares and serve.

If you plan on freezing one pan, allow the second pan to cool completely. Then wrap it tightly in another sheet of aluminum foil and freeze it for up to 3 months. Defrost in the refrigerator and reheat in the oven.

Frittata di Vermicelli Senza Uove
Vermicelli Pie Without Eggs

Luigi DiMajo Norante, owner of DiMajo Norante winery in Campomarino, Molise, is a busy man who takes great pleasure in cooking. In the time it takes to set the table, he is sitting down to enjoy his no-egg vermicelli frittata with a glass of one of his classic DiMajo Norante wines. The dish is also good made with leftover pasta. Be sure to lightly oil the pan before cooking the frittata; that is the secret to its coming out perfect every time without sticking.

Serves 4 to 6

¼ cup extra-virgin olive oil
1 large garlic clove, peeled and chopped
1 tablespoon capers in salt, rinsed and minced
2 anchovies in olive oil, drained and chopped
½ teaspoon dried hot red pepper flakes
½ pound vermicelli or spaghetti, cooked
½ cup grated Parmigiano-Reggiano cheese
¼ cup minced flat-leaf parsley

Heat a 10-inch nonstick sauté pan over medium heat. Pour in the olive oil, add the garlic, and cook until the garlic softens. Stir in the capers, anchovies, and hot pepper flakes. Cook 2 minutes. Add the vermicelli and stir it well into the ingredients. Stir in the cheese and the parsley. Lower the heat and cook until the underside is brown and crisp, about 5 minutes. Place a dish wider than the sauté pan over the top of the frittata and flip it out. If the pan is dry, add a teaspoon of oil. Return the frittata to the pan to cook the other side. Slide the frittata onto a serving dish and cut it into wedges.

Linguine al Limone e Panna
Linguine with Lemon and Cream

Maybe you need only enough pasta for one or two people. Treat yourself to this zippy linguine with lemon, ham, and Parmesan cheese.

Saving time: Grate enough cheese to store in the refrigerator. Grated zests can be frozen and kept in small sandwich bags for future use. Invest in a Microplane zester, available in kitchen stores and online.

Serves 2

---

2 tablespoons butter

4 thin slices of prosciutto or ham, cut into strips

½ cup canned low-sodium chicken or vegetable broth

Grated zest of 1 lemon

2 tablespoons lemon juice

4 tablespoons heavy cream or nonfat half-and-half

Coarse black pepper to taste

½ cup grated Parmigiano-Reggiano cheese

¼ pound linguine

Melt the butter in a 12-inch sauté pan. Ad the prosciutto or ham and cook for 1 minute. Pour in the broth and cook 1 minute longer. Stir in the lemon zest and juice. Stir in the cream and cook over low heat for 2 minutes. Add black pepper to taste. Keep the sauce covered and warm while the linguine is cooking.

Cook the linguine according to the directions on pages 40–41.

Transfer the linguine to the pan with the sauce; stir well over medium heat. Stir in the cheese. Transfer the linguine to a serving platter. Serve hot.

Schiaffoni al Forno con Salsa di Asparagi
Oven-Baked Smacks with Asparagus Sauce

Carlo Fusco is so passionate about pasta that he is a master designer, dreaming up several new shapes each day for the Colavita Pasta Company. I visited him in Vinchiaturo in Molise, a region that is known for its superior dried pasta. It was fascinating to watch the process of how hard wheat semolina flour and water mixed together resulted in some very fancy pasta shapes. One of Carlo's favorites is *schiaffoni*, meaning "smacks." It is a rather large tubular pasta similar to manicotti shells and is best cooked *al forno* (baked). If you cannot find this shape, use large manicotti or cannelloni shells. This dish is lip-smackingly good with an unusual asparagus sauce.

Serves 8

¼ cup grated pecorino or Parmigiano-Reggiano cheese

1 tablespoon extra-virgin olive oil

⅓ pound diced pancetta

1¼ pounds asparagus, tough stems removed and stalks cut into thirds

1 cup sliced portobello mushrooms

1 cup fresh peas

1 cup prepared Pesto Sauce (page 62)

1 pound schiaffoni

2 hard-boiled eggs, coarsely chopped

Extra-virgin olive oil as needed

Fine sea salt as needed

Preheat the oven to 350°F.

Sprinkle the cheese into a 9 × 12 × 2-inch-deep casserole dish or use 2 smaller casserole dishes. Set aside.

Heat the oil in a sauté pan. Stir in the pancetta and cook until it begins to brown. Stir in asparagus pieces and cook until they soften, about 3 or 4 minutes. Stir in the mushrooms and cook until the mushrooms give off their liquid. Stir in the peas and the pesto sauce. Keep the sauce warm while the pasta cooks.

Cook the schiaffoni for 5 minutes, drain, and place it in a single layer in the prepared casserole dish or dishes. Spread the sauce over the pasta and sprinkle the egg over the sauce. Drizzle the top with olive oil. Cover the pan with aluminum foil and bake it for 15 minutes.

Spaghetti con Tonno, Capperi e Limone
Spaghetti with Tuna, Capers, and Lemon

Canned tuna in olive oil teamed with peas, onions, capers, and fresh lemon juice is a sauce that explodes with flavor, and is a must-have favorite when teamed with pasta for a quick supper. The components for this dish came from my stay in the fishing village of Mondello, Sicily, where the life of a fisherman is always on display. Walking along the shoreline reveals a chorus line of colorful tuna and swordfish boats painted in brilliant red, green, and blue stripes. As they bob up and down to the rhythm of the waves, fishermen sell their catch, singing out in a wild dialectic cadence while they mend their long expanses of intricately woven fish nets. The trick to this recipe is to use the best canned tuna in olive oil. I prefer the Marinella brand.

Saving time: Make and refrigerate the tuna sauce a day or two ahead.

Serves 8

---

1 medium onion, peeled and quartered

2 garlic cloves, peeled

3 tablespoons capers in brine or salt, rinsed well and drained

2 (6-ounce) cans solid tuna in olive oil or 1 (10.5-ounce) jar Marinella brand
   tuna in olive oil

1 teaspoon (or more) hot red pepper flakes

1½ teaspoons dried oregano

Salt to taste

Coarse black pepper to taste

2 tablespoons fresh lemon juice

1 pound plain or whole wheat spaghetti or bow ties
¼ cup reserved cooking water
2 tablespoons minced flat-leaf parsley

Let your food processor do the work of mincing together the onion, garlic, and capers. The mixture should be very fine. No processor? Mince everything together by hand using a chef's knife.

Pour 1 tablespoon of the olive oil from the jar or can of tuna into a large sauté pan. Reserve the rest. Heat the oil, stir in the minced mixture, and cook until the onion softens. Stir in the red pepper flakes and the tuna with all of the oil. Flake the tuna with a fork and continue to cook over medium heat for 2 minutes. Stir in the oregano, salt, pepper, and lemon juice. Set aside and keep the mixture warm or, if making this sauce ahead, transfer it to a jar and refrigerate it. When ready to use, simply reheat.

Cook the spaghetti or bow ties as described on pages 40–41. Drain, reserve ¼ cup of the cooking water, and transfer the pasta and reserved water to the sauté pan. Raise the heat to medium high and stir everything together until heated through. Sprinkle on the parsley and serve.

Spaghetti Spezzati con Gamberi
Broken Spaghetti with Shrimp

Breaking long cuts of spaghetti and linguine in half not only makes it easier to eat, but it cooks faster as well, and when you are in a hurry this is a way to save time. This audacious shrimp dish comes together fast when frozen cooked shrimp and spinach or broccoli are on hand. The inspiration for it comes from the region of Molise, where the use of hot red peppers, *il diavulill* (the devil), signifying hotness, is so much a part of Molisana cooking.

Serves 8

---

1 teaspoon (or more) dried hot red pepper flakes

1 large garlic clove, peeled

2 tablespoons flat-leaf parsley

1 tablespoon fresh mint leaves

Zest and juice of 1 lemon

Salt to taste

1 pound frozen medium-size cooked shrimp, defrosted

2 teaspoons extra-virgin olive oil

1 cup frozen chopped broccoli or spinach, defrosted and squeezed dry

6 cherry tomatoes, cut in half

1 pound spaghetti or other long pasta, broken in half

¼ cup reserved cooking water

Coarse black pepper to taste

Mince the red pepper flakes, garlic, parsley, and mint together. Transfer the mixture to a bowl. Stir in the zest and lemon juice and a pinch of salt. Toss the shrimp in the mixture and allow it to stand for 5 minutes.

Heat the olive oil in a large sauté pan. When the oil is hot, stir in the shrimp and cook 2 minutes. Stir in the broccoli or spinach and cook 1 minute more. Stir in the tomatoes and cook 1 minute longer. Keep the mixture warm.

Cook the spaghetti according to the directions on pages 40–41.

After draining the spaghetti, add it to the shrimp along with the reserved water and reheat quickly until everything is hot. Correct the seasoning with salt and pepper and serve.

Pronto Sauces

Salsa Aglio e Olio (Garlic and Oil Sauce)

Pesto (Classic Basil Sauce)

Ragù Napoletano alla Anna Galasso (Grandma Anna Galasso's Neapolitan Meat Sauce)

Salsa di Finocchio e Pomodorini (Roasted Fennel and Cherry Tomato Sauce)

Salsa di Noci (Walnut Sauce)

Salsa di Pomodoro (Tomato Sauce)

Salsa di Pomodoro Crudo (Uncooked Tomato Sauce)

Here are seven easy sauces that I use all the time. They can be mixed and matched to dress pasta but they are also good with fish, vegetables, and meats. But hold on to your apron because there are so many sauces in the Italian kitchen that it would be impossible to fill a book. Why? Because sauces are an invention of every cook. There just are no formalized sauces, no textbook versions. Here is a good example: In an Italian kitchen, a cook may have a few zucchini on hand, olive oil and garlic, an onion or two and some fresh herbs, let's say oregano. The zucchini is diced, the garlic and onion minced, and everything goes into a pot with the olive oil, oregano, salt, and pepper. A few minutes later, sauce.

Most people think of sauces as something in a liquid state, but in the Italian kitchen a sauce can be chunky, fine, in between, or hardly there, as is the case for *Salsa Aglio e Olio* (Garlic and Oil Sauce), page 61.

All the sauces in this chapter can be made ahead of time and either frozen or refrigerated.

Salsa Aglio e Olio
Garlic and Oil Sauce

If there is a sauce more classic than tomato it has got to be *Aglio e Olio*, garlic and oil, and who does not have those healthful ingredients on hand? This sauce exudes comfort. It is what I crave when I want something light, something that is not an assault on my stomach, and something that just plain puts me in a good mood. This sauce is sheer perfection and really is a great example of using the best ingredients for tasty results. Use a good, fruity, extra-virgin olive oil, fresh garlic, and fresh parsley. It is that simple. The recipe makes enough to dress 12 ounces of spaghetti or linguine. The recipe can be doubled to serve more.

Saving time: Buy bunches of fresh flat-leaf parsley, mince them fine, divide into 4-tablespoon batches and wrap tightly in a paper towel, folding it like an envelope, and freeze in small sandwich bags. That way it is always on hand.

Makes 1 cup

¾ cup fruity extra-virgin olive oil
2 garlic cloves, peeled and finely minced
1 teaspoon salt
Coarse black pepper to taste
⅓ cup minced flat-leaf parsley leaves

Heat the olive oil slowly in a pot. When it begins to shimmer at the edges, stir in the garlic and cook it, pressing on it with a wooden spoon until the garlic begins to brown. Take care not to let it burn or you will have to start over. Turn off the heat and stir in the salt, pepper, and parsley. Simple, ready, and good.

Pesto
Classic Basil Sauce

Many sauces today are marketed as pesto and have such names as tomato pesto, parsley pesto, and arugula pesto. But the classic will always be pesto sauce made from fresh basil leaves, pine nuts, garlic, oil, and cheese. There are times when you might think that it is just more convenient to yank a jar of sauce off the supermarket shelf. But convenience may not be all that you are getting. How about lots of preservatives, additives, and megadoses of salt! A homemade pesto can avoid all those, and is not time consuming to make if you use a food processor. This dense sauce is great not only on pasta but also brushed on grilled salmon or grilled tomatoes. It is wonderful mixed into a hot potato salad and equally at home as a topping for pizza. A little goes a long way; ½ cup is enough to coat 12 ounces of pasta.

Makes 1¼ cups

---

2 cups packed fresh basil leaves, stems removed

2 garlic cloves, peeled

⅓ cup pine nuts or walnut pieces

½ to ⅔ cup extra-virgin olive oil

Salt to taste

Coarse black pepper to taste

¼ cup grated pecorino or Parmigiano-Reggiano cheese

Pulse the basil leaves, garlic, and pine nuts together in a food processor until the mixture is coarse-looking. I like texture but if you want it smoother, pulse longer. Pour the olive oil through the feed tube while the motor is running. As soon as the sauce is well blended, stop the machine and wipe down the sides of the bowl with a rubber spatula. Transfer the mixture to a small bowl and stir in the salt and pepper. If using immediately, stir in the cheese. Otherwise stir in the cheese just before serving.

Pour the pesto into a jar, leaving about ¼ inch at the top, and pour in a thin layer of olive oil. This will prevent air from getting into the pesto and turning the color from green to brown. Cap and refrigerate the pesto for up to 2 weeks. Bring the pesto to room temperature before using.

Note: *When stirring pesto into hot pasta, mix it first in a small bowl with ¼ cup of the pasta cooking water. This will help to thin out and smooth the sauce.*

Ragù Napoletano alla Anna Galasso
Grandma Anna Galasso's Neapolitan Meat Sauce

A typical Neapolitan ragù is a meat sauce made with beef or pork or a combination of both and cooked slowly with tomatoes. This was the sauce that simmered in a large pot for hours on the back burner on Sunday morning while my family went to mass. When we returned home, the smell of it permeated the house, and we could hardly wait to have that plate of macaroni mixed with a sauce that was so flavorful and sweet-tasting that we wiped our plates clean with a slice of bread to mop up any left-behind driblets. This is a great do-ahead sauce; it can be made 4 or 5 days before using and it can also be frozen for months. This is my grandmother Anna Galasso's recipe, the one she carried with her in her head all the way from Avellino, Italy, to her new home in America.

🕐 **Saving time:** Make this sauce on the weekend and freeze some for future use. Use a food processor to mince and chop the vegetables.

Makes 8 cups

1½ pounds top round steak, cut ⅛ inch thick

Salt

Coarse black pepper

⅓ cup minced flat-leaf parsley

¼ cup grated pecorino cheese

4 meaty spareribs on the bone

2 tablespoons extra-virgin olive oil

1 onion, peeled and coarsely chopped

1 celery rib, coarsely chopped

1 large carrot, coarsely chopped

2 large garlic cloves, peeled and minced

1 bunch of fresh basil leaves, torn into pieces

3 (28-ounce) cans crushed plum tomatoes

½ cup dry red wine

1 tablespoon salt

Coarse black pepper to taste

1 tablespoon sugar

Dry the round steak with paper towels and rub it on both sides with salt and pepper. Sprinkle the meat with the parsley and cheese.

Roll the meat up like a jelly roll and tie it in several places with kitchen string. Salt and pepper the spare ribs. Set the meats aside.

Pour the olive oil into a 4-quart heavy-duty pot. Over medium heat brown the round steak and spare ribs well in the oil on all sides. This will take about 5 minutes.

Stir in the onion, celery, and carrot and continue cooking until the vegetables begin to soften. Stir in the garlic and basil. Cook 1 minute.

Combine the tomatoes and wine in a bowl. Slowly pour the mixture over the meat. Stir in the tablespoon of salt, pepper, and the sugar. Cover the pot, bring the sauce to a boil, then lower the heat to simmer. Cook the sauce until the meat is fork tender, about 1½ hours.

Remove the meat to a dish. Cover the dish and refrigerate the meat to make it easier to cut. When ready to use, transfer the round steak to a cutting board and cut off the string with a kitchen scissors. Cut the meat into neat slices about ½ inch thick. Cut the meat off the bones of the spareribs.

Preheat the oven to 300°F. Place the meats in a casserole dish and cover with some of the sauce. Cover the casserole with aluminum foil and warm the meats in the oven.

Use the sauce over pasta and serve the meats as a second course.

Note: *The sauce (with the meat) can be frozen in batches for future use for lasagne, pasta dishes, with vegetables such as green beans, zucchini, and eggplant, and over pizza.*

Salsa di Finocchio e Pomodorini
Roasted Fennel and Cherry Tomato Sauce

When is a sauce not just a sauce? When it can be used as a side vegetable dish, or even as a topping for pizza. You will get three variations with this fix-it-and-forget-it roasted fennel and cherry tomato sauce. The exquisite flavor is due to one key ingredient . . . sugar.

Makes about 1¾ cups

2 tablespoons extra-virgin olive oil

1 large fennel bulb (about 12 ounces), washed, bulb part only thinly sliced into rings

2 pints cherry tomatoes, washed

3 garlic cloves, peeled and cut in half lengthwise

½ teaspoon salt

2 teaspoons sugar

Preheat the oven to 350°F.

Brush a 12-inch baking pan with the olive oil. Add all the ingredients to the pan and toss them well to coat them in the oil. Put the pan in the oven and bake for 20 to 25 minutes, stirring occasionally, just until the vegetables have softened.

Use the sauce to dress ¾ pound of spaghetti or short-cut macaroni like ziti or penne. Or use it as a topping for pizza, over baked fish, or as a side dish. However you use it, it is delicious!

Variation: Add a tablespoon of minced capers at the end of the cooking to give the sauce a nice sweet-and-sour taste. Two tablespoons of fresh thyme is another refreshing variation.

Salsa di Noci
Walnut Sauce

This sauce is so versatile: Use it for whole wheat pasta or as a sauce over grilled fish, pork, and chicken. It's equally good on cooked green beans and sautéed cherry tomatoes. The whole thing is zip, zip fast in the food processor, and the sauce will keep for a week or more in the refrigerator.

Makes 1 ¼ cups

1 cup walnut halves
1 garlic clove, peeled
1 cup packed flat-leaf parsley
½ cup fat-free half-and-half
½ teaspoon salt
Coarse black pepper to taste
⅓ cup grated pecorino cheese
1 tablespoon extra-virgin olive oil

Pulse the nuts, garlic, and parsley in a food processor until almost smooth; it should have some texture. Pour the mixture into a bowl and stir in the half-and-half, salt, pepper, and lastly the cheese. Spoon the sauce into a jar and pour a thin film of olive oil over the top. Cap and refrigerate.

To use on cooked pasta, bring 1 cup of the sauce to room temperature and stir into 1 pound of cooked, hot pasta. To use on fish, spread a generous tablespoon on top of the fish just before serving. Or mix a tablespoon or two into cooked green beans.

Salsa di Pomodoro
Tomato Sauce

You can make a great-tasting tomato sauce in less than 25 minutes. It takes longer than that to go to the grocery store and buy a jar, bring it home, and reheat it! If you have canned plum tomatoes, fresh garlic, olive oil, and basil, you are on your way to raves. Use this sauce for pasta, on pizza, to mix into stews, in calzones, for stewing vegetables such as zucchini, in stuffed vegetables, for making lasagne . . . need I say more?

Makes 2½ quarts

¼ cup extra-virgin olive oil
2 garlic cloves, peeled and minced
3 (28-ounce) cans crushed plum tomatoes
½ cup red wine
Salt to taste
Coarse black pepper to taste
1 bunch of fresh basil leaves, torn into pieces
1 tablespoon sugar

Heat the olive oil in a 3-quart pot. When the oil begins to shimmer, stir in the garlic and cook it over medium heat until it begins to soften. Do not let it brown. Lower the heat and stir in the tomatoes, wine, salt, pepper, basil leaves, and sugar. Bring the sauce to a boil, then lower the heat to simmer, cover the pot, and cook 20 minutes.

To freeze for future use, let the sauce cool, pour it into heavy-duty plastic bags, and freeze.

Salsa di Pomodoro Crudo
Uncooked Tomato Sauce

There is tomato sauce and then there is uncooked tomato sauce, the perfect topper for short cuts of pasta like penne or ziti. But this sauce can also be used to top crusty toasted bread slices for a great summertime bruschetta. Or plop a spoonful over grilled chicken or pork chops. The trick is to use really great-tasting tomatoes, so making this sauce in the summertime is ideal when tomatoes are bursting off the vines. For less than stellar tomatoes, cheat and add a teaspoon or two of sugar to the sauce. No one will ever know.

Makes 2 cups

½ cup extra-virgin olive oil

2 garlic cloves, peeled

7 large fresh basil leaves, stemmed

¼ cup tightly packed flat-leaf parsley leaves

4 or 5 meaty plum tomatoes

½ teaspoon salt

Coarse black pepper to taste

Sugar (optional)

Pour the olive oil into a bowl and set aside. Make a pile on a cutting board of the garlic, basil, and parsley. Mince with a chef's knife or put the ingredients into a food processor and pulse a few times until they are minced.

Stir the garlic mixture into the olive oil.

Dice the tomatoes and add them to the olive oil with the salt and pepper and a little sugar, if need be. Mix well. Cover the bowl and allow the mixture to marinate several hours at room temperature before using.

The sauce can also be made a few days ahead of time and stored in the refrigerator. Bring to room temperature before using.

To use on pasta, cook the pasta as directed on pages 40–41. Toss the pasta while hot with the sauce and serve immediately.

Pass grated cheese on the side, if desired.

Variation: Add ½ cup diced oil-cured olives, artichokes, or peppers to the sauce.

Pronto Main Dishes

Bistecca alla Pizzaiola (Beefsteak with Tomato Sauce)

Scaloppine con Salsa di Gorgonzola (Veal with Gorgonzola Sauce)

Costolette di Maiale al Rosmarino (Skillet Breaded Pork Chops with Rosemary)

Maiale alla Griglia con Salsa di Marmellata (Grilled Pork Tenderloin with Orange
    Marmalade Sauce)

Pollastra al Forno con Patate e Pomodori (Rock Cornish Game Hens with Potatoes and
    Tomatoes)

Pollo con Olive (Chicken with Olives)

Pronto Pollo alla Cacciatore (Quick Hunter-Style Chicken)

Pollo Dieci Minuti (Ten-Minute Chicken)

Tacchino alla Napoletana (Turkey with Tomato and Mozzarella)

Pesce Fritto con Mandorle e Parmigiano-Reggiano (Fried Fish Fillets with Almond and
    Parmesan Cheese Coating)

Salmone con Vermicelli al Cartoccio (Steamed Salmon with Vermicelli in Parchment)

Tonno, Carciofi, Capperi e Ceci (Fresh Tuna with Artichokes, Capers, and Chickpeas)

Frittata di Spaghetti (Fried Spaghetti Omelet)

Tuttoinsieme (Mixed-Up Vegetables)

econdi are main entrées of meat, fish, poultry, game, and vegetarian dishes that are served after the *primi* (first course) of soup, pasta, rice, or polenta. I have so many quick favorites from my travels that it was hard to decide what to tempt you with. I wanted something comforting in the mix, so my all-time favorite spaghetti frittata is definitely one that you should try, as well as fellow chef Jasper White's unbelievably crisply fried fish, decidedly Italian, with its crunchy almond and parmesan cheese coating. Chicken cacciatore is always a winner, especially with children. My version is bright and flavorful with juicy chunks of boneless breast simmering in just a hint of a spicy tomato sauce. Need something for company? The scaloppine in gorgonzola sauce will have you licking the pan, and you can make it in no time at all just before the doorbell rings. And who does not like turkey? Dress it up Neapolitan style with tomatoes, mozzarella cheese, and basil. Treat yourself and others to cool fresh tuna, artichoke, capers, and chickpeas as a salad on a hot summer's day, then serve it hot over pasta when the weather turns cold.

Mix and match these dishes with those in the soups or pasta chapter or serve them with a fresh field greens salad.

Bistecca alla Pizzaiola
Beefsteak with Tomato Sauce

Anytime you see the word *pizzaiola* you can assume that the dish is made Neapolitan style with tomatoes, oregano, and garlic, as in this delicious, thin-sliced sirloin steak *pizzaiola*, ready in no time at all when you keep tomato sauce on hand.

Serves 4

1 pound boneless sirloin steak, thinly sliced
Salt to taste
Coarse black pepper to taste
3 tablespoons unsalted butter
1 teaspoon dried oregano
2½ cups prepared Tomato Sauce (page 69)
⅓ cup minced flat-leaf parsley

Season the meat on both sides with salt and pepper.

Melt the butter in a large sauté pan over medium-high heat. Sauté the meat, in batches if necessary, on both sides until lightly browned. Sprinkle the meat with the oregano. Stir in the tomato sauce and simmer the mixture for 5 minutes. Stir in the parsley and serve.

Variation: Veal, pork, or chicken cutlets also work well in this recipe.

Scaloppine con Salsa di Gorgonzola
Veal with Gorgonzola Sauce

Scaloppina means a thinly pounded slice of meat, usually veal. This dish is so elegant that no one will know it took you only minutes to prepare. The success depends on the cut of the veal. It should be meat from the top round, not the leg, which is tough and not suited for this dish. The sauce is a cinch to make with gorgonzola cheese that is either *dolce* (sweet, younger cheese) or the more sharply pronounced and aged gorgonzola *forte*.

🕐 **Saving time:** Have butcher pound the veal slices for you.

Serves 4 to 6

1½ pounds veal cutlets, ⅛ inch thick, cut from the top round

Salt to taste

3 tablespoons unsalted butter

5 ounces gorgonzola dolce (or forte) cheese, cut into bits

1 cup fresh or frozen and defrosted peas

1 teaspoon grated lemon zest

Radicchio leaves for garnish

Sprinkle the veal slices with a little salt and set aside.

Over medium heat melt the butter in a sauté pan large enough to hold all the slices, or cook them in batches. Quickly brown the slices on both sides. Transfer them to a dish and keep them covered and warm while making the sauce.

Reduce the heat to low and stir in the cheese until it is melted. Stir in the peas and lemon zest and heat through.

Arrange the radicchio leaves around the outside of a serving platter. Place the veal slices in the center and pour the sauce over them. Serve immediately.

Variation: Add diced tomatoes to the sauce after the cheese has melted. Use chicken or pork as a substitute for veal.

Costolette di Maiale al Rosmarino
Skillet Breaded Pork Chops with Rosemary

These rosemary-flavored breaded pork chops get a little kick from fresh hot red pepper.

Saving time: A thinner cut of pork saves cooking time. Use Egg Beaters rather than whole eggs to avoid spending time beating eggs.

Serves 4

2 teaspoons diced hot red pepper or 1 teaspoon dried flakes
2 garlic cloves, peeled and minced
2 tablespoons minced fresh rosemary needles
2 teaspoons salt
Coarse black pepper to taste
1 cup toasted bread crumbs
⅓ cup Egg Beaters or 2 large eggs, slightly beaten
8 center-cut bone-in pork chops, ½ inch thick
4 tablespoons extra-virgin olive oil
Lemon wedges

Mix the red pepper, garlic, rosemary, salt, pepper, and bread crumbs on a sheet of wax paper. Set aside.

Pour the Egg Beaters or beaten eggs into a shallow dish. Dip the chops in the egg on both sides, then coat each one on both sides in the bread-crumb mixture, pressing them in with your hands. Transfer them to a dish. Do not stack them on top of each other. Refrigerate the chops, uncovered, for 10 minutes.

Heat the olive oil in an oven-to-table sauté pan. Brown the chops on both sides over medium heat for about 3 minutes on each side. Do them in batches, if necessary, keeping them warm as you brown them. Serve immediately with lemon wedges.

Maiale alla Griglia con Salsa di Marmellata
Grilled Pork Tenderloin with Orange Marmalade Sauce

Pork (*maiale*) is revered in Italy, and the Italians really know how to cook it, as in their beloved *porchetta* (spit-roasted whole suckling pig), and how to cure it for prosciutto. Try this easy grilled pork tenderloin, a favorite of my husband, Guy, who came up with this recipe. He serves it with a very quick-to-make balsamic vinegar and orange marmalade sauce. This most tender cut is elegant, moist, and tangy. A great company choice that is stress-free!

Serves 8

2 whole pork tenderloins, about 1¼ pounds each
Fine sea salt
Coarse black pepper to taste
1 (8-ounce) jar orange marmalade
¼ cup commercial balsamic vinegar

Preheat an outdoor grill to 450°F.

Wash and dry the tenderloins well with paper towels. Rub them with fine sea salt and coarse black pepper and set aside.

Make the sauce in a small saucepan. Heat the marmalade with the balsamic vinegar and stir until the sauce is smooth. Remove ⅓ cup of the sauce to use for basting the tenderloins. Cook the remaining sauce over low heat for 3 to 4 minutes. Keep the sauce warm and covered.

Place the tenderloins on the grill. Baste them quickly with the sauce and cook them for 7 minutes over indirect heat with the grill top closed. Lower the heat to

375°F., turn the tenderloins, and and baste them again. Close the grill and cook an additional 5 minutes. Turn off the grill and allow the meat to sit for another 5 minutes. Following this method will result in juicy and not overcooked meat.

Transfer the tenderloins to a cutting board. Cover them loosely with aluminum foil and allow them to stand 5 minutes.

Cut the pork on the diagonal into 1-inch slices; arrange them on a platter, and serve, passing the remaining sauce on the side.

Variation: Add a tablespoon of fresh chopped rosemary to the finished sauce.

Pollastra al Forno con Patate e Pomodori
Rock Cornish Game Hens with Potatoes and Tomatoes

Chef Gianfranco Campanella is a first-generation Italian-American. Even though he was born here, his family moved back to Sicily when he was a boy, and that's where he developed his love of Italian cooking. His father was in the restaurant business, and Gianfranco honed his skills by his side, and is now the corporate chef at Mediterraneo in Providence, Rhode Island's Little Italy on Atwells Avenue. When he is not working, he likes to put together easy dishes at home. This preparation of savory Rock Cornish game hens with potatoes and tomatoes is worthy of company.

Serves 4

---

2 Rock Cornish game hens, each about 1 pound, 5 ounces
½ cup flour
1 teaspoon salt
½ teaspoon freshly ground black pepper
½ cup extra-virgin olive oil
1 medium red onion, peeled and thinly sliced
1 cup dry white wine
3 medium red potatoes, washed and cut into wedges
1 (16-ounce) can peeled tomatoes or 8 fresh plum tomatoes, peeled*
2 garlic cloves, peeled and smashed
Needles from 1 fresh rosemary sprig

* To peel tomatoes, bring a pot of water to the boil, turn off heat, and add tomatoes. Remove them after 10 or 20 seconds. The skins should slip right off.

Leaves from 2 fresh thyme sprigs

6 basil leaves, torn into large pieces

Salt to taste

Coarse ground pepper to taste

Preheat the oven to 400°F.

Rinse and dry the game hens. With a sharp chef's knife, cut them in half and then into quarters.

Combine the flour, salt, and pepper in a zip-lock bag. Place the pieces in the bag and shake to coat them well. Transfer the pieces to a dish.

Put a large roasting pan on the stove. You may need to use two burners. Add the olive oil and heat it until the oil begins to shimmer. Add the pieces and brown them well on all sides. As they brown, transfer them to a dish. Set aside.

Add the onion to the pan and cook it until it begins to brown; turn off the heat. Pour in the wine and add the potatoes, tomatoes, garlic, rosemary, thyme, and basil. Season everything with salt and pepper.

Place the game pieces on top of the vegetables. Cover with aluminum foil and bake 1 hour and 15 minutes.

Uncover and serve with some of the vegetables and pan juices.

Pollo con Olive
Chicken with Olives

For this lively-tasting, country-style olive-and-chicken dish that is so typical of the region of Abruzzi and Molise, you can do all the marinade preparations the night before. Working with marinades means thinking ahead, and that is what is so great about them.

🕐 **Saving time.** Use a mini food processor to coarsely chop the olives, garlic, and herbs together. Keep peeled garlic cloves tightly wrapped in plastic wrap in the refrigerator.

Serves 4

½ cup pitted green olives

2 garlic cloves, peeled

1 tablespoon fresh sage leaves

1 tablespoon fresh rosemary needles

1 teaspoon salt

Coarse black pepper to taste

Pinch of ground nutmeg

Zest and juice of 2 large lemons

3½ pounds cut-up chicken pieces

¾ cup dry red wine

1 sweet red bell pepper, seeded and cut into thin strips

Coarsely chop together the olives, garlic, sage, and rosemary. Transfer the mixture to a shallow baking dish large enough to hold the chicken pieces (a 9 × 12-inch pan).

Stir in the salt, pepper, and nutmeg. Stir in the zest and lemon juice. Add the chicken pieces and turn to coat them in the mixture. Cover and refrigerate overnight.

When ready to cook, heat the olive oil in a sauté pan large enough to hold the chicken in a single layer. Brown the pieces well on both sides. Raise the heat to high and stir in the wine. Cook 2 minutes. Reduce the heat to medium-low, cover the pan, and cook 30 minutes. Add the peppers during the last 5 minutes of cooking.

Serve the chicken hot with some of the pan juices.

Pronto Pollo alla Cacciatore
Quick Hunter-Style Chicken

Chicken cacciatore, hunter-style chicken, tastes better made a day or two ahead. Cut-up, bone-in pieces of chicken are usually used, but here is a version ready in less than 30 minutes. The secret? Using boned chicken breasts cut into strips to speed the cooking time.

⏱ **Saving time:** Buy chicken breasts in quantity, cut them into strips, and freeze for future use. They will defrost more quickly, too. Onions and garlic can be minced in batches, wrapped well in plastic wrap, and also frozen for future use.

Serves 4 to 6

1¼ teaspoons salt

1 teaspoon celery seeds

1¼ teaspoons dried oregano

¼ teaspoon freshly ground black pepper

1 teaspoon hot red pepper flakes, or more

6 boned chicken breast halves, cut into 2-inch-wide strips

2 tablespoons extra-virgin olive oil

1 onion, peeled and minced

3 garlic cloves, peeled and minced

2 celery ribs, thinly sliced

1 medium green pepper, seeded and diced

⅓ cup white wine

1 (28-ounce) can tomatoes

Juice of 1 lemon

Combine the salt, celery seeds, oregano, pepper, and pepper flakes in a plastic bag. Add the chicken strips, close the bag, and shake to coat them in the mixture.

Heat the olive oil in a sauté pan large enough to hold the breast strips in a single layer. If you don't have a large enough pan, brown them in batches.

Brown the strips on both sides and transfer them to a dish. Add the onion, garlic, celery, and green pepper to the pan and cook until the mixture softens.

Raise the heat to high, pour in the wine, and allow most of it to evaporate. Lower the heat and stir in the tomatoes and lemon juice. Return the chicken strips with their juices to the pan. Cover and simmer the mixture for 15 minutes. Use immediately or refrigerate. Reheat slowly.

Variation: Packaged sliced mushrooms make a nice addition, as does 1 cup frozen peas. Add the mushrooms with the celery; add the peas 5 minutes before the chicken is done.

Pollo Dieci Minuti
Ten-Minute Chicken

Cooking for one or two? Just open your pantry, get out those staples, and in five minutes or less prep time, this rustic chicken dish is ready to pop into the oven. Even better, get it all together the night before and bake the next day. I call it *pollo dieci minuti* (ten-minute chicken) because that is how long it will take to cook. The key is to use chicken tenders, strips of chicken cutlet that are cut about 4 inches long and 1½ inches wide. Find them in the meat section of your supermarket.

Saving time: Mince the basil, rosemary, and garlic in a food processor.

Serves 2

---

3 tablespoons extra-virgin olive oil

1 teaspoon dried oregano

2 tablespoons minced fresh basil

1 tablespoon minced fresh rosemary needles

1 garlic clove, peeled and minced

¼ teaspoon dried red pepper flakes

½ teaspoon fine sea salt

Coarse black pepper to taste

1 pound chicken tenders (4 × 1½ inches wide)

Preheat the oven to 350°F.

Pour the olive oil into a 9 × 10 or 12-inch casserole dish. Stir in the oregano, basil, rosemary, garlic, pepper flakes, salt, and pepper.

Add the chicken pieces and turn them in the herb mixture so that they are well coated.

Bake uncovered for 10 to 12 minutes.

Serve hot.

Tacchino alla Napoletana
Turkey with Tomato and Mozzarella

Tacchino (turkey) is not as popular in Italy as it is here, but this dish takes on a Neapolitan flair when fresh mozzarella cheese (*fior di latte*), ripe plum tomatoes, and spicy basil are part of the mix.

Serves 4 to 6

---

2 pounds cooked turkey, cut into ¼-inch-thick slices
2 tablespoons extra-virgin olive oil
Salt to taste
Coarse black pepper to taste
1½ cups sliced fior di latte (cow's milk mozzarella) cheese
3 large plum tomatoes, thinly sliced
¼ cup chopped fresh basil

Preheat the oven to 350°F.

Brush a large shallow baking dish with 1 tablespoon olive oil. Place the turkey in 1 layer in the dish and season the pieces with salt and pepper. Lay the cheese evenly over the pieces and overlap the tomatoes on top of the cheese. Sprinkle on the basil and drizzle the remaining olive oil evenly over the top.

Bake for 20 minutes or just until the cheese has melted.

Pesce Fritto con Mandorle e Parmigiano-Reggiano
Fried Fish Fillets with Almond and Parmesan Cheese Coating

No one knows or cooks fish better than chef Jasper White, who credits his Italian heritage for his approach to serving straightforward, wonderful fish in his restaurant, the Summer Shack. I love his almond-and-parmesan-encrusted flounder fillets. They fry up crispy and juicy. Chef Jasper finishes off the dish with a squirt of lemon juice and some tomato wedges on the side.

Saving time: Make the bread-crumb mixture several days ahead and refrigerate.

Serves 4

Almond and Parmesan Bread Crumbs

Makes 1½ cups

½ **cup sliced almonds, coarsely chopped**
½ **cup grated Parmigiano-Reggiano cheese**
½ **cup panko bread crumbs***
½ **teaspoon kosher or sea salt**
¼ **teaspoon freshly ground black pepper**

* Panko are large, flaked Japanese bread crumbs found in your grocery store in the Oriental foods aisle or in the gourmet food aisle. They are perfect for coating fish and hold up well in frying, creating a nice crunchy texture.

1 pound flounder fillets

Sea salt

Freshly ground black pepper

2 whole eggs, lightly beaten

1 tablespoon water

1 cup unbleached all-purpose flour

3 tablespoons olive oil, plus more if needed

4 tablespoons butter, plus more if needed

Lemon and tomato wedges

Combine the first five ingredients well in a shallow bowl. Set aside.

Line a large platter with paper towels and set aside.

Halve the flounder fillets lengthwise and check for bones. Season lightly with salt and pepper.

Crack the eggs into a bowl and beat them well with the water.

Spread the flour in a shallow bowl.

Dredge the fillets in the flour and shake off the excess.

Dip them 1 at a time in the egg wash and coat them well. Then coat them well with the bread crumbs. Place the fillets in a single layer on a platter.

Put an empty 12-inch sauté pan over medium heat for 5 minutes.

Add the olive oil and butter so that it completely coats the pan and the mixture is is hot. When the butter is bubbling and beginning to brown, add half the fillets to the hot oil mixture. Let them fry evenly for about 2 minutes. If they begin to brown before that, turn down the heat.

Flip the fillets in the direction away from you. Let them pan-fry for another 2 minutes until crisp and golden brown. Remove pan from the heat and use a slotted spatula to transfer the fish to the paper-lined platter. Add more oil and butter to the pan, if needed, to cook the remaining fillets.

Serve hot with lemon and tomato wedges.

Salmone con Vermicelli al Cartoccio
Steamed Salmon with Vermicelli in Parchment

Many upscale Italian restaurants impress their guests with fish cooked *al cartoccio*, or steamed in parchment paper or aluminum foil. You can, too. This technique is both functional and tasteful, because wrapping the ingredients seals in the juices and putting this dish together is effortless, yet the result is elegant. Let the drama unfold the next time you have company and take the high road to make this exotic *pesce al cartoccio*. For added interest and presentation, place the fish on a bed of cooked vermicelli (thin pasta) before closing up the paper or foil.

Saving time: Cook and refrigerate the vermicelli up to two days ahead.

Serves 4

4 tablespoons extra-virgin olive oil

2 cups cooked plain vermicelli

2 tablespoons fresh lemon juice

1 teaspoon salt

2 teaspoons minced fresh thyme

2 teaspoons minced flat-leaf parsley

1 tablespoon Dijon mustard

4 salmon fillets, 6 ounces each

1 small onion, peeled and diced

1 small zucchini, diced

6 cherry tomatoes, cut in half

½ cup bottled clam juice or dry white wine

Preheat the oven to 450°F.

Cut four 10 × 12-inch sheets of parchment paper or aluminum foil and set aside. Have a baking sheet ready.

Use 1 tablespoon of the oil to brush the four sheets of foil or parchment paper. Set aside.

Mix the vermicelli in a bowl with the remaining 3 tablespoons oil. Divide and spoon it into the center of each sheet.

Mix the lemon juice, salt, thyme, parsley, and mustard together in a small bowl. Brush each fish fillet with some of the mixture and place 1 fillet on top of each pile of vermicelli. Sprinkle the onion, zucchini, and tomatoes evenly over the top of each fillet. Pour 2 tablespoons of the clam juice or wine over each.

Bring the four corners of the parchment or aluminum foil up and twist the ends together to form a bundle. Place them on the baking sheet.

Bake for 10 to 12 minutes. The salmon should remain moist and the color of coral in the center. Do not overcook.

Place a package on each of 4 dinner plates and serve at once, letting each guest open his or her own package. You can stand back and watch the steam and smiles escape.

Variation: Clams or mussels in their shells or a combination of both are good for this recipe, too.

Tonno, Carciofi, Capperi e Ceci
Fresh Tuna with Artichoke, Capers, and Chickpeas

Fresh tuna with fennel, artichokes, chickpeas, and capers evokes many memories of days spent in sunny Sicily's lively Vuccaria market, where fishmongers draw you to their colorful stalls with their shrill sounds of salesmanship. Whole swordfish and tuna are the most impressive. Make this dish early in the day or a day ahead to allow the flavors to complement one another.

🕐 **Saving time:** Poach and refrigerate the tuna ahead of time.

Serves 4

½ pound fresh tuna steak

1 bay leaf

1 lemon, thinly sliced

1 teaspoon coarse sea salt

1 (10-ounce) package frozen artichoke hearts

1 cup canned chickpeas, drained and rinsed

½ cup diced fennel or celery

½ cup diced red onion

2 tablespoons capers in salt, rinsed well, dried, and minced

¼ cup minced flat-leaf parsley

⅓ cup extra-virgin olive oil

2 tablespoons white vinegar

Place the tuna steak in an 8-inch sauté pan and just barely cover it with cold water. Add the bay leaf, lemon slices, and salt. Bring the water to just under a simmer and cook the fish slowly until it turns uniformly gray. This will take about 5 or 6 minutes. Drain the tuna, transfer it to a large bowl, and flake it with a fork into large pieces. Let it cool.

Put the artichokes in a small saucepan, add ½ cup cold water, and bring them to a boil. Cook until tender, about 4 minutes. Drain and coarsely chop them. Add them to the bowl with the tuna. Stir in the chickpeas, fennel or celery, onion, capers, and parsley. Toss the ingredients well. Pour the olive oil over all and toss. Sprinkle the vinegar over the mixture and toss again. Add additional salt if necessary.

Serve at room temperature.

Variations: add hard-boiled egg slices and minced black oil-cured olives.

Make a hot main dish by combining this recipe with 12 ounces cooked spaghetti or linguine.

Frittata di Spaghetti
Fried Spaghetti Omelet

In Italian, *fare una frittata* means to make a mess of things. Making leftover spaghetti into a frittata, a fried omelet, is a perfect example of how to create leftover magic and use up a mess of things in your refrigerator like bits of ham, leftover vegetables, mushrooms, or cooked meats. It was done all the time in Italian kitchens of long ago as a meal stretcher and still is. I always regarded it as a special treat, not as a leftover. This classic is the answer to that age-old question, "What's for supper?" Even if you don't have leftover spaghetti, a package or two is on your pantry shelf waiting to be cooked.

Serves 4 to 6

4 large eggs
2 tablespoons minced fresh herbs such as flat-leaf parsley, thyme, or basil
Salt to taste
¾ cup diced cheese, whatever you have
½ cup leftover vegetables, cooked meats, mushrooms, or other ingredients
2 cups leftover spaghetti, sauced or plain
2 tablespoons extra-virgin olive oil

Beat the eggs with a whisk in a medium-size bowl just until they are foamy. Stir in the herbs, salt, cheese, leftover vegetables, and meats. Stir in the spaghetti. Set aside.

Heat the oil in an 8- or 10-inch nonstick sauté pan over medium heat. When the oil is hot, carefully pour in the spaghetti mixture and smooth it with a spatula. Cover the pan and cook until the egg mixture begins to firm up and the frittata moves in one piece when the pan is shaken. Lift up one end of the frittata with a spatula, and if it looks lightly browned, slide it out onto a dish. Turn it over and slip it back into the pan to cook the other side. Transfer it to a serving dish and cut it into wedges.

Tuttoinsieme
Mixed-Up Vegetables

I take inspiration from the healthful Italian diet that has always included a bevy of fresh vegetables. I call this dish *Tuttoinsieme* (everything together), a sort of vegetarian "chili" that was created when I was cleaning out the refrigerator. Out came half of a zucchini and a small summer squash. A couple of celery stalks that were starting to go limp were added to the pile, and an onion. I got to work. By adding some spices, diced tomatoes, and wheat berries, I had a meal that was tasty and nutritious. Sometimes the best things come from the hidden confines of your refrigerator. This is a great do-ahead recipe to make with kids on the weekend and will keep beautifully in the refrigerator for a few days; make it in batches and freeze it. It is even good as a sauce over pasta.

Serves 4 to 6

2 tablespoons extra-virgin olive oil

1 small onion, peeled and diced

2 celery stalks, diced

1 small zucchini, cubed

1 small summer squash, cubed

1 teaspoon celery salt

1 teaspoon celery seed

1 teaspoon dried oregano

2 tablespoons minced fresh thyme

Salt to taste

Coarse black pepper to taste

1 cup chopped button mushrooms

1 (28-ounce) can diced tomatoes with their juice

1 cup canned kidney beans, rinsed and drained, or 1 cup cooked wheat berries, orzo, or rice

Grated Parmigiano-Reggiano cheese for sprinkling

Pour the olive oil into a medium-size soup pot and add the onion, celery, zucchini, and summer squash. Cook together, covered, over medium heat until the vegetables soften, about 4 minutes. Sprinkle them with the celery salt, celery seed, oregano, thyme, salt, and black pepper. Stir in the mushrooms and continue cooking until the mushrooms soften. Pour in the tomatoes. Cover and cook for 15 minutes. Add the beans, wheat berries, orzo, or rice. Stir well. Serve in bowls and sprinkle with cheese.

LEFTOVERS PRONTO

We have all had this experience: cleaned out the refrigerator only to find some mysterious covered container with slime-green leftovers we meant to use up a month before! I guess that old adage is right: If it is out of sight, it is out of mind, and in this case, ripe with mold.

I'll bet there are leftovers lurking in your refrigerator right now that you are planning to use up . . . sometime. Right now you just can't think about eating the same thing twice in one week, and you don't have any ideas on how to create something new with them. So there they sit. Let's take some likely leftover foods as examples and create a framework to see what they could become the next day or day after. But don't expect me to give you exact recipes because that would negate what leftovers can become, culinary knockoffs off the top of your head. If you just incorporate a new technique, leftover foods can become something completely gourmet. Here are several ideas to get you thinking creatively about them.

Suppose baked fish was your last night's meal and you still have a good portion on hand. What can you do with it? Well, you might want to just reheat it and have a dried-out ho-hum leftover supper. There is no magic in that. Instead, why not flake the fish in a bowl with a fork, add an egg, salt, pepper, a little chopped parsley, and a dash of hot sauce. Take small amounts in your hands and form the mixture into patties. Coat them in bread crumbs and fry them in a little vegetable oil. Now you have fish cakes, a whole new look and taste.

How about that leftover pot roast or pork roast? Slice the meat off the bone into thin strips. In a sauté pan, cook some onion in a little olive oil with some minced garlic; stir in some green beans and cook them just until they begin to soften. Transfer them to a plate. Throw in a handful of mushrooms and cook them until softened. Add them to the plate with the green beans. Now turn up the heat and stir in the meat. Give it a dash of red or white wine and when it is hot, return the beans and mushrooms to the pan and heat everything until it's hot. Serve it as is or with cooked rice, leftover polenta, or pasta.

Leftover chicken? Cube the meat and make chicken salad with chunks of apples, some diced celery, shaved carrots, and a few walnuts. Make a vinaigrette with olive oil, rice wine vinegar, and salt. Throw in a few herbs like tarragon, basil, or parsley if you have them.

We all have leftover vegetables from time to time, and they are easy to turn into omelets and crustless quiches. Just combine them with eggs and cheese, a few herbs, and bake.

Leftover pasta combined with some herbs, cheese, and leftover vegetables like broccoli and spinach takes on a whole new form when it gets turned into a great frittata. Check out the one on page 98.

Leftover mashed potatoes can be mixed with cooked spinach, some bits of ham or sweet peppers, and baked in the oven like a potato pie. Or combine the potatoes with an egg, some minced parsley, salt, and pepper and form into small balls. Coat the balls in bread crumbs and fry them quickly in a little canola oil. They make a great side dish.

Cooked squash can double for the mashed potato suggestion as well. Or make soup out of the squash by diluting it with enough canned or homemade low-sodium chicken broth until it is of the consistency you like. Stir in a little nutmeg and a touch of half-and-half, and a creamy soup is yours in no time. Garnish the top with bread croutons made from leftover stale bread.

And speaking of bread, remember that wonderful bread pudding you loved as a child? That was born from leftovers, too.

What these examples demonstrate is that leftovers deserve a second chance and can be pretty exciting, fast, and chic.

Pronto Vegetables and Salads

Insalata Caprese (Neapolitan Stack Salad)

Insalata all' Alessio DiMajo (Alessio DiMajo's Salad)

Insalata di Cesare (Caesar Salad)

Insalata di Radicchio e Pera (Radicchio and Pear Salad)

Insalata di Finocchio, Radicchio e Arance (Fennel, Radicchio, and Orange Salad)

Insalata di Valeriana con Prosciutto e Formaggio (Spring Salad with Ham and Cheese)

Insalata di Verdure Miste Arrostite con Scamorza (Mixed Roasted Vegetable Salad with Scamorza Cheese)

Insalata Rinforzata (Sicilian Cauliflower Salad)

Broccolo al Forno (Oven-Roasted Cauliflower)

Gattò di Patate (Neapolitan Potato Pie)

Parmigiano di Melanzane e Zucchine (Layered Eggplant and Zucchini Casserole)

Peperoni Ripieni con Riso e Formaggio (Cubanelle Peppers Stuffed with Rice and Cheese)

Pomodorini con Porri e Timo (Cherry Tomatoes with Leeks and Thyme)

Fagiolini con Salsa di Pomodoro (Green Beans in Tomato Sauce)

Pomodori in Padella con Formaggio e Pangrattati (Skillet Tomatoes with Cheese and Bread Crumbs)

Italians are dedicated vegetable connoisseurs. Their outdoor markets form a cornucopia of colors with crates brimming with everything imaginable. They crave bitter greens such as radicchio, arugula, and dandelions for salads; they love marinated vegetables, especially anything *scapece* style, such as thin slices of eggplant and zucchini marinated in olive oil and vinegar. They are geniuses at making savory stuffings with bread crumbs and cheese for vegetables like artichokes and sweet bell peppers. In southern Italy the ubiquitous *peperoncino*, hot red pepper, fresh or dried, is never far from the hands of the cook.

The easiest cooking technique is *alla griglia*, which means vegetables that are grilled and simply brushed with olive oil and lightly seasoned with salt. Above all, the tomato, more than any other vegetable (it's really a fruit), defines southern Italian cooking and put Italy on the culinary map.

The recipes in this chapter showcase traditional and innovative ways to prepare a variety of vegetables, from something as simple and savory as Green Beans in Tomato Sauce to sweet Oven-Roasted Cauliflower.

Insalata Caprese
Neapolitan Stack Salad

When the term *caprese* is applied to food, it means in the style of the sunny island of Capri, an idyllic island south of the Bay of Naples. *Insalata Caprese* is probably one of the most recognizable salads in the Italian repertoire. Fresh and creamy buffalo mozzarella cheese, made in areas around Naples, slightly greenish tomatoes, and the freshest basil are the components. It looks impressive when everything is stacked together and simply dressed with the best extra-virgin olive oil and red wine vinegar.

Serves 4

---

4 large plum tomatoes, each cut into 4 slices

2 (8-ounce) balls buffalo mozzarella or fior di latte cheese, each cut into 8 slices

16 whole basil leaves, stemmed

6 tablespoons extra-virgin olive oil

4 teaspoons red wine vinegar

1 teaspoon salt

On a platter make 4 stacks using 4 slices of tomatoes, 4 slices of mozzarella, and 4 basil leaves for each stack. Begin with a tomato slice, top it with a mozzarella slice, then a basil leaf, and repeat the process to make 3 more layers in each stack.

In a small bowl whisk the oil with the vinegar and salt and drizzle it over the stacks.

Serve immediately.

Insalata all' Alessio DiMajo
Alessio DiMajo's Salad

Simple, elegant, delicious, and effortless. This stunner of a salad, made with romaine lettuce, fresh buffalo mozzarella balls, and whole cherry tomatoes, was put together for me by vintner Alessio DiMajo, who with his father, Luigi, makes some pretty impressive DiMajo Norante wines in the region of Molise. What is so astounding about the dish is the way the salad is arranged and the quality of the ingredients used. It comes together in no time at all and will make a statement for your next dinner party. The recipe can be adjusted up or down. Substitute *fior di latte* (cow's milk mozzarella) for the buffalo mozzarella.

Serves 8

2 very fresh heads romaine lettuce
16 small whole balls of fresh mozzarella (fior di latte) cheese
16 whole cherry tomatoes
1 small bunch basil leaves
Fine sea salt
Extra-virgin olive oil

Cut off the core ends of the heads of lettuce and separate the leaves. Use the whole inner leaves since they are crisper. Wash and dry them. You will need 8 leaves for this recipe. Line a large round platter with the leaves in a circular pattern so that the bottom ends point to the center of the platter.

Place 2 mozzarella balls in the center of each of the leaves. Add two cherry tomatoes at the top of each leaf. Arrange the bunch of basil in the center of the platter.

Pass the platter and allow each person to take one of the romaine leaves and some of the basil.

Pass the salt and olive oil on the side.

Insalata di Cesare
Caesar Salad

Caesar salad has nothing to do with the Roman emperor Julius Caesar. It was the twentieth-century innovation of Italian immigrant Caesar Cardini, who made the original salad for a group of Hollywood actors. The salad was said to contain coddled eggs, lemon juice, olive oil, grated Parmesan cheese, croutons, salt, and pepper. There were no anchovies. Here is my twist on this classic, which contains poached eggs and thin Parmesan wafers. Use hearts of romaine; the inner leaves are necessary for the great crunch of this salad. This is a quick, impressive, complete light supper or lunch dish combining protein, vegetables, and fiber.

🕐 **Saving time:** Keep a plastic container of grated Parmigiano-Reggiano cheese and a bag of washed and dried lettuce in the refrigerator.

Serves 4

---

1 cup grated Parmigiano-Reggiano
2 anchovies in salt, rinsed (optional)
4 tablespoons light mayonnaise
Salt to taste
Coarse black pepper to taste
1 tablespoon freshly squeezed lemon juice
4 cups hearts of romaine lettuce, washed, spun dry, and torn into pieces
4 large eggs
Extra grated Parmigiano-Reggiano cheese for sprinkling

Place a nonstick 8-inch skillet over medium heat for 2 minutes. Spread ¼ cup of the cheese into a 3-inch diameter in the pan. Cook the cheese until it begins to bubble and brown around the edges. Carefully slip a metal spatula under the cheese and remove it to a plate lined with paper towels. Make 3 more cheese circles.

In a small bowl mash the anchovies with a fork and combine them with the mayonnaise. (Or eliminate the anchovies). Test for saltiness; if you like more, add it. Stir in a good grinding of the pepper and the lemon juice. Set aside.

Place the lettuce in a salad bowl. Toss the salad with the dressing and arrange on each of 4 salad plates. Place a cheese round at the edge of each plate. Set aside.

Fill a 1-quart pot half full with water and bring it to a boil; reduce the heat and allow the water to come back to a simmer.

Crack each egg separately into a small bowl. Slip them carefully, 1 at a time, into the water and poach gently for 2 minutes or until the egg white is set. Remove the egg with a slotted spoon. Place the egg in the center of the salad greens and serve immediately. Pass the extra parmesan cheese for sprinkling over the salad.

Insalata di Radicchio e Pera
Radicchio and Pear Salad

Insalate now come in many new guises in Italy, where, in times past, mixed greens or greens with raw vegetables was the acceptable and traditional norm. But isn't it nice to flirt with tradition and add some new twists? This colorful and refreshingly different radicchio salad would be considered *alta cucina* (gourmet cooking) on the Italian table.

Serves 4

2 ripe Anjou, William, or Bosc pears, cored and thinly sliced

1 tablespoon lemon juice

2 small heads radicchio, torn into small pieces

½ cup broken walnut pieces

⅓ cup dried cranberries

1 blood or naval orange, peeled and separated into segments

¼ cup crumbled gorgonzola dolce cheese

Dressing

⅓ cup white balsamic vinegar or rice wine vinegar

½ cup extra-virgin olive oil

¼ teaspoon fine sea salt

¼ teaspoon celery seed

1 tablespoon honey

Place the pears in a shallow bowl and combine them with the lemon juice. Cover and set aside.

Whisk the dressing ingredients together in a small bowl and set aside.

Combine the radicchio, walnuts, cranberries, and orange segments in a bowl. Pour the dressing over the top and toss well. Add the pears with the lemon juice and toss again.

Sprinkle the top with the cheese and serve.

Variation: Dried figs, chopped, instead of cranberries make a nice alternative.

Insalata di Finocchio, Radicchio e Arance
Fennel, Radicchio, and Orange Salad

This jewel of a salad is made with fennel, that licorice-tasting celery that is an essential ingredient in Italian cooking. Look for it in the produce department. You will recognize it by its white bulbous base and feathery leaves. Toss it with red radicchio (a slightly bitter chicory) and sweet blood orange segments. This salad is perfect after a fish course or for a change of pace.

Saving time: Salad greens like radicchio can be found in the produce section already washed, separated, bagged, and ready to use.

Serves 4

¼ cup pine nuts
¼ cup extra-virgin olive oil
2 tablespoons red wine vinegar
½ teaspoon fine sea salt or to taste
Coarse black pepper to taste
1 small fennel bulb, washed, dried, and thinly sliced
1 small head radicchio, washed, dried, and torn into pieces
2 large blood or navel oranges, peeled, segmented, and cut in half

Toast the pine nuts in a small skillet over medium heat just until they begin to brown, about 2 minutes. Transfer the nuts to a small bowl. Set aside.

Combine the olive oil, vinegar, salt, and pepper in a jar. Set aside. Toss the fennel, radicchio, and oranges in a salad bowl. Pour the dressing over the salad and mix well. Sprinkle the pine nuts over the top and serve.

Insalata di Valeriana con Prosciutto e Formaggio
Spring Salad with Ham and Cheese

Insalata di Valeriana is a refreshing spring salad made with small, tender greens similar to mache, also called lamb's ear lettuce. I first enjoyed *valeriana* at Ristorante L'Incontro, near Modena, where chef Gianfranco Zinani serves it with fine strips of prosciutto cooked in balsamic vinegar, then adds Parmigiano-Reggiano cheese chips and cherry tomatoes. Substitute fresh baby spinach if mache is unavailable. Make this delicious salad a part of a company meal, a nice diversion from just a mixed green salad.

Serves 4

¼ pound prosciutto or cooked ham, cut into thin strips

1 tablespoon balsamic vinegar

2 cups washed and dried mache or baby spinach

1½ tablespoons extra-virgin olive oil

½ teaspoon fine sea salt

¼ cup Parmigiano-Reggiano, in small chips

6 cherry tomatoes, cut in half

In a small pan, cook the prosciutto strips in the balsamic vinegar, stirring to coat the prosciutto well. Let the vinegar evaporate. Transfer the strips to a dish and set aside.

Toss the mache or baby spinach in a bowl with the olive oil and the salt. Add the prosciutto, cheese, and tomatoes. Toss gently and serve.

Insalata di Verdure Miste Arrostite con Scamorza
Mixed Roasted Vegetable Salad with Scamorza Cheese

Inspiration for many of my recipes comes from my observations of what's available in regions of Italy that I visit. Molise and Campania are two of my favorites, where you can be sure to get some of the best artisanal cheeses like buffalo mozzarella and *scamorza*. *Scamorza* is a cow's milk cheese similar in texture to mozzarella and takes its name from its pear or "dunce-cap" shape. It is tied around the top with string and when smoked has a brown rind.

Saving time: Make the dressing and cube and refrigerate the cheese several days ahead. Seed, cut into chunks, and refrigerate the peppers a day ahead.

Serves 4 to 6

Dressing

⅓ cup extra-virgin olive oil

Juice of 2 large lemons

3 tablespoons minced fresh thyme

1 teaspoon fine sea salt to taste

Coarse black pepper to taste

½ teaspoon sugar

2 tablespoons extra-virgin olive oil

1 small eggplant, stemmed, cut into ½-inch-thick rounds and quartered

1 small cauliflower head, separated into 1-inch florets

1 large red pepper, seeded and cut into 1-inch chunks

1 large yellow pepper, seeded and cut into 1-inch chunks

6 garlic cloves, peeled

12 spring onions, bulbs only, left whole

6 cherry tomatoes, cut in half

6 yellow cherry tomatoes, cut in half

½ cup cubed scamorza or mozzarella cheese

Preheat the oven to 375°F.

Combine the dressing ingredients in a small jar and aside.

Spray a baking sheet with olive oil. Toss the eggplant, cauliflower, peppers, garlic, and onions together in a large zip-lock bag with 2 tablespoons olive oil. Spread the vegetables on the baking sheet and roast them for 10 minutes, or just until the eggplant begins to soften and the cauliflower begins to brown. Turn the vegetables once during the cooking time.

Transfer the vegetables to a large bowl. Add the tomatoes and cheese and gently toss everything with the dressing.

Transfer the vegetables to a serving platter. Serve at room temperature.

Variation: Adding canned chickpeas or cannellini beans boosts the protein in this salad.

Insalata Rinforzata
Sicilian Cauliflower Salad

Cauliflower mixes well with a variety of raw vegetables especially in a colorful Sicilian *insalata rinforzata* (reinforced salad), so named because even when it is a leftover, you can add things from the refrigerator like carrots, leftover peas, asparagus, and so forth to give it new taste nuances.

Serves 6 to 8

1 medium head cauliflower, outer stems and core removed
½ cup extra-virgin olive oil
2 garlic cloves, peeled and minced
4 tablespoons red wine vinegar
½ cup diced green or black oil-cured olives
¼ cup diced red onion
½ cup diced sweet red pepper
¼ cup chopped flat-leaf parsley
2 tablespoons capers in brine, drained and minced
½ cup diced tomatoes or ¼ cup diced sun-dried tomatoes in
    olive oil
1 cup canned chickpeas, drained and well rinsed
Salt to taste

Have a pot of boiling salted water ready on the stove.

Break the cauliflower into small uniform-size florets. Add them to the boiling water and cook 1 minute. Drain well and transfer the florets to a salad bowl.

Add the olive oil, garlic, wine vinegar, olives, onion, pepper, parsley, capers, tomatoes, and chickpeas to the cauliflower. Add salt to taste and toss well. Cover with plastic wrap and allow the salad to marinate at room temperature for 30 minutes. Or make it ahead, refrigerate overnight, and bring it to room temperature to serve.

Broccolo al Forno
Oven-Roasted Cauliflower

Cauliflower is one of the most beloved vegetables of Sicily, where it is affectionately known as *broccolo*. (Broccoli as we know it is called *sparaceddi* in Sicily.) The pale green cauliflower heads make a colorful statement piled high in carts along Sicily's road-sides, waiting for savvy cooks to snap them up and add them to pasta and salad dishes. A convenient way for you to cook it is to roast the florets, which brings out a mild, sweet taste.

🕐 **Saving time:** No time to clean and separate the cauliflower into florets? Buy them already separated and cleaned in packages in the produce department of your grocery store.

Serves 6 to 8

---

1 medium head cauliflower
⅓ cup extra-virgin olive oil
2 teaspoons celery salt
1 teaspoon salt
Coarse black pepper to taste
2 teaspoons minced fresh thyme

Preheat the oven to 350°F.

Turn the cauliflower upside down on a cutting board and cut around the center core. Discard the core and separate the cauliflower into 1-inch florets. Wash and dry them and set aside.

In a large bowl combine the olive oil, celery salt, salt, pepper, and thyme.

Add the florets and toss them well. Spread them on a baking sheet and bake them for 20 to 25 minutes, turning them once or twice, until they begin to brown and the stems are easily pierced by a fork. Serve as a side dish with meat, pork, or fish.

Gattò di Patate

Neapolitan Potato Pie

Gattò di Patate is a savory Neapolitan potato pie that makes a wonderful side dish for chicken or meat. It can be made with fresh or leftover mashed potatoes and bits of cheeses and cured meats that you may have in your refrigerator. Floury potatoes work best in this dish.

Saving time: Use a microwave to bake the potatoes, and to soften the butter if it is cold. Keep grated cheeses on hand in the refrigerator to save a step in this recipe.

Serves 6 to 8

---

4 large baking potatoes (2¼ pounds), scrubbed, or 4 cups leftover mashed potatoes

4 tablespoons unsalted butter, softened (2 tablespoons if using leftover mashed potatoes)

2 eggs, slightly beaten

⅓ cup milk

½ cup grated Parmigiano-Reggiano cheese

¼ cup grated pecorino cheese

¼ pound diced ham

3 tablespoons minced flat-leaf parsley

4 slices provolone cheese, diced

5 ounces mozzarella cheese (fior di latte), diced

⅓ cup bread crumbs (optional)

2 tablespoons unsalted butter, melted (optional)

Butter a 9 × 9 × 2-inch baking dish and set aside.

Preheat the oven to 350°F.

Bake the potatoes in their skins in the microwave according to the manufacturer's directions. Cool and peel.

Mash the potatoes in a large bowl until smooth. Stir in 4 tablespoons of the butter. If you are using leftover mashed potatoes, use only 2 tablespoons butter. Combine the eggs and milk in a small bowl and blend them into the potatoes. Stir in the Parmigiano-Reggiano and pecorino cheeses. Stir in the ham and parsley.

Spread half the mixture in the pan. Sprinkle the diced cheeses over the potatoes. Cover with the remaining mashed potato mixture.

Sprinkle the bread crumbs over the top if using. Drizzle the remaining 2 table-spoons of butter over the bread crumbs and bake the pie for about 45 minutes, or until the top is nicely browned. Serve hot.

Variation: Use thin slices of plum tomatoes instead of bread crumbs and butter for the topping.

For a lighter version of this dish, use only the egg whites; beat them until soft peaks form and then fold them into the potato mixture.

Parmigiano di Melanzane e Zucchine
Layered Eggplant and Zucchini Casserole

Strips of eggplant and zucchini stacked with cheese and tomato sauce make a great vegetarian "lasagne" main or side dish. And the best part is that there is no coating of the vegetables in egg and bread crumbs and no frying!

🕐 **Saving time:** A mandoline is a great tool for making even slices, strips, or julienne cuts of vegetables.

Serve 6

Olive oil spray
1 medium eggplant (1 pound), washed, dried, and stemmed
2 large zucchini (1 pound), washed, dried, and stemmed
2½ cups prepared Tomato Sauce (page 69)
½ pound provolone cheese, shredded
1 cup grated Parmigiano-Reggiano cheese

Preheat the oven to 375°F.

Spray 2 baking sheets with olive oil.

Cut the eggplant and zucchini lengthwise into ¼-inch-thick slices with a sharp knife, or use a mandoline, following the manufacturer's instructions.

Make a single layer of eggplant on one baking sheet and one of zucchini on the other. Spray the tops with olive oil and bake them for about 5 minutes or just until the slices soften.

Meanwhile, spread a thin layer of tomato sauce on the base of a 9 × 12-inch baking dish.

Make a layer of softened eggplant in the base of the dish. Spread ¼ cup of the tomato sauce over the slices and sprinkle them with 2 tablespoons each of the provolone and Parmigiano-Reggiano cheeses. Top with a layer of zucchini slices and another ¼ cup of tomato sauce. Sprinkle 2 more tablespoons each of the cheeses over the top. Repeat and make 2 more layers, ending with the zucchini. Spread the remaining sauce and cheeses over the top.

Cover the dish tightly with aluminum foil and bake for 25 minutes or until heated through. Remove from the oven and allow the dish to stand for 5 minutes before cutting into squares.

Serve hot.

Peperoni Ripieni con Riso e Formaggio
Cubanelle Peppers Stuffed with Rice and Cheese

Sweet peppers, hot peppers, dried peppers—they all define southern Italian cooking. They are revered by cooks, who grill, pickle, and stuff them in so many ways. *Cornetti* are long, green peppers found in Italy that are similar to our more readily available cubanelle or banana peppers. This is the Italian frying pepper that is light green in color but matures to red when left to ripen. They are stuffed with grated cheese and arborio rice, the same type of rice used to make risotto but without all that stirring. This is a colorful side dish presentation for meats, fowl, or fish. The peppers can also stand on their own as a meal in themselves.

Serves 4

---

4 red or green banana or cubanelle peppers about 5 inches long and 3 inches wide

1 cup arborio rice

1¾ cups chicken broth

1 cup grated aged caciocavallo, pecorino, or provolone cheese

¼ cup minced flat-leaf parsley

1 teaspoon fine sea salt

Coarse black pepper to taste

2 tablespoons extra-virgin olive oil

Preheat the oven to 375°F.

Lightly grease an 8- or 9-inch-square baking dish with olive oil and set aside

Cut the stem top off each pepper and reserve it. Use a small spoon to remove the seeds from the inside of the peppers.

Make a small hole at the end of each pepper with a toothpick to prevent them from splitting when baked.

Put the rice in a 1-quart saucepan. Pour in the broth and bring to a boil. Lower the heat to medium low, cover the pot, and cook the rice until it is al dente, meaning still firm but cooked through. Drain the rice in a colander and transfer it to a bowl. Stir in the cheese, parsley, salt, pepper, and 1 tablespoon of the olive oil. Mix to combine the ingredients. Divide and stuff the rice into each pepper cavity.

Place the peppers on their sides in the baking dish. Replace the stem tops. Drizzle the remaining olive oil over the peppers.

Cover the dish tightly with aluminum foil and bake the peppers for 30 minutes. Uncover them and bake for 10 minutes or until they are tender.

Serve at room temperature.

Pomodorini con Porri e Timo
Cherry Tomatoes with Leeks and Thyme

Cherry tomatoes seem to have nine lives. They are great for salads, wonderful popped into stews and soups, make great stuffed antipasto bites, and are fabulous as a side dish with leeks and thyme. Leeks (*porri*) were revered by the Romans, who ate them for health benefits. This is minimalist cooking—when a few choice ingredients combine to create something succulent.

Serves 4

1 medium leek
2 tablespoons extra-virgin olive oil
1 pound cherry tomatoes, rinsed
2 teaspoons minced fresh thyme
1 teaspoon fine sea salt
1 tablespoon sugar

Leeks tend to harbor a lot of dirt. Cut off the dark green tops and the root end and discard them. Cut the leek lengthwise down the center. Rinse well under cold water. Dry and dice.

Heat the olive oil in a sauté pan. Stir in the leek and cook until it is wilted. Stir in the cherry tomatoes and cook just until they begin to wrinkle and soften. Stir in the thyme, salt, and sugar and continue cooking for 2 or 3 minutes. Serve hot or at room temperature.

Variation: Sprinkle the mixture with toasted pine nuts or crumbled gorgonzola dolce cheese before serving.

Fagiolini con Salsa di Pomodoro
Green Beans in Tomato Sauce

Green Beans in Tomato Sauce is a classic recipe from home. Every time I make it, I see my Neapolitan grandmother in her flowered apron with a small green mountain of beans spread out on newspaper on the kitchen table. One by one she trimmed them and piled them into a large colander. She used green beans in so many ways. Beans with mint, olive oil, and vinegar for a salad was a favorite, as was this dish of beans mixed with homemade tomato sauce.

🕐 **Saving time:** Keep tomato sauce on hand in the freezer.

Serves 4 to 6

1½ pounds green beans, trimmed

2 teaspoons salt

2 cups hot prepared Tomato Sauce (page 69)

Rinse the beans and put them into a soup pot. Add the salt and cover the beans with cold water.

Bring them to a boil and cook them, uncovered, just until a small knife is easily inserted; they should remain al dente.

Drain the beans and transfer them to a serving bowl. Pour the sauce over the beans, stir well, and serve.

Variation: Add ½ cup cubed mozzarella cheese to the beans before mixing with the sauce.

Pomodori in Padella con Formaggio e Pangrattati
Skillet Tomatoes with Cheese and Bread Crumbs

Skillet tomatoes topped with melted cheese and crunchy bread crumbs make a great side dish, an easy antipasto, or a light lunch. They look impressive as part of a buffet spread.

Saving time: Keep a container of toasted bread crumbs in the refrigerator. They have a long shelf life.

Serves 4

3 tablespoons extra-virgin olive oil

1 garlic clove, peeled and minced

⅔ cup bread crumbs

1 teaspoon dried oregano

¼ teaspoon fine sea salt

4 large plum tomatoes, cut in half, turned upside down on paper towels and allowed to drain

1 cup shredded provolone or mozzarella cheese (fior di latte)

4 slices toasted bread (optional)

Heat the olive oil in a sauté pan, add the garlic, and cook until the garlic just begins to brown. Stir in the bread crumbs and "toast" them until they are golden brown. Transfer the crumbs to a small bowl; stir in the oregano and salt.

Return the pan to the stove and cook the tomatoes, cut side down, over medium-low heat for about 3 minutes or just until they begin to soften and shrink. Don't overcook them or they will collapse and lose their shape. Turn the tomatoes cut side up.

Sprinkle the cheese evenly over the tomatoes. Cover the pan and allow the cheese to melt.

Sprinkle some of the bread crumb mixture over the top of each half.

Serve immediately as is or on top of toasted bread slices.

Pronto Tramezzini

La Pasta Base (Basic Yeast Dough)

Calzoni Pronti (Calzones with Sausage and Peppers)

Panino Favorito della Mamma (Mom's Favorite Chicken Cutlet and Broccoli Rabe Sandwich)

Ciabatta con Salame e Parmigiano-Reggiano (Flat Bread with Salami and Parmesan Cheese)

Panini di Scamorza, Peperoni e Carciofi (Scamorza Cheese, Sweet Peppers, and Artichoke Sandwiches)

Pizza Margherita (Classic Pizza with Fresh Tomatoes, Mozzarella, and Basil)

Polenta (Cooked Cornmeal)

Rotolo di Broccoletto (Stuffed Broccoli Rabe Roll)

Tramezzini is a lyrical, catchy word for small sandwiches, the kind Italians munch on at a local bar while taking an interlude, a pause in the day. Now, a sandwich is not hard to put together. Most of us probably eat more of them than anything else because they are quick, transportable, and filling. But the ingredient that makes an Italian sandwich get all the attention and craving is great bread. Supermarkets and bakeries have heard the call. We want better bread: European artisanal breads such as crusty whole wheat; flat and chewy *ciabatta*; tangy sourdough types like Tuscan bread; and flat bread like focaccia. And more people are interested in making their own bread, so be sure to try the easy recipe for Basic Yeast Dough on page 137.

Besides bread, the filling ingredients must be top notch. For Italians this means foods such as *prosciutto di Parma*, classic cheeses like *mozzarella di bufala*, provolone, *scamorza*, and *caciocavallo*. It means great dry-cured salami and roasted vegetables such as eggplant and red peppers. It means quality extra-virgin olive oil and fresh herbs like spicy basil. The best news is that these ingredients are available in your grocery store or Italian deli.

Try Tomie dePaola's *ciabatta* bread with salami, olive oil, and Parmigiano cheese on page 142. Classic and superior ingredients make this sandwich a joy to eat, and it's a snap to put together. There is also my mother's favorite sandwich, chicken cutlet with sautéed broccoli rabe and melted cheese, and the impressive *Rotolo di Broccoletto*, stuffed bread dough with cheese and broccoli rabe, which can be considered anything from a gourmet sandwich to a main course to part of an antipasto. Try all the *tramezzini* in this chapter; they are unusual, easy, and delicious, and they are not just for lunch anymore.

La Pasta Base
Basic Yeast Dough

Making a yeast dough from scratch for pizza, rolls, bread, or focaccia couldn't be simpler when done in a food processor. Easy does it with the flour; add just enough to make a ball of dough that is not sticking to your fingers. Too much flour will result in a heavy dough. No food processor? Make it by hand in a large bowl. Once it rises, the dough can be punched down and frozen in lightly oil-sprayed zip-lock plastic bags for up to 2 months.

Makes 1 pound, 14 ounces

1¾ cups warm water (110°F.)
1 package active dried yeast (0.25 ounce)
1 tablespoon extra-virgin olive oil
4 to 4½ cups unbleached all-purpose flour
2 teaspoons salt

Position the dough blade in a food processor. Pour in the water and add the yeast. Whirl the mixture to dissolve the yeast. Add the olive oil, 4 cups of the flour, and the salt and whirl to make a dough. Add some of the remaining flour if the dough is soupy or very sticky; you have enough flour when the dough wraps around the blade and releases from the sides of the bowl.

Transfer the dough to a lightly oiled bowl. Cover tightly with plastic wrap and allow it to rise until double in size. This could take from 45 minutes to 1 hour. When it has risen, punch the dough down with your fists and use it to make the rotolo di broccoletto (page 150), form it into a loaf of bread, or use it for pizza, calzones, bread sticks, or pizza fritta.

Calzoni Pronti
Calzones with Sausage and Peppers

Calzones are trendy turnovers. I consider them unique sandwiches. They are a little fancier-looking and great for a party or picnic or just a diversion from the ordinary. Fillings can be just about anything, from this spicy sausage-and-tomato combination to vegetarian offerings. Using store-bought pizza dough delivers good eating in no time at all.

🕐 **Saving time:** Make the filling several days ahead; keep a supply of pizza dough and tomato sauce in the freezer. Use a food processor to chop and dice the vegetables and garlic. Assemble and freeze the unbaked calzones ahead.

Makes 8

¾ pound sweet Italian sausage, casing removed

1 small red bell pepper, seeded and chopped

1 small yellow bell pepper, seeded and chopped

1 garlic clove, peeled and minced

1 small red onion, peeled and chopped

1½ teaspoons fennel seeds

1 cup diced mozzarella cheese

Salt to taste

Ground black pepper to taste

½ cup Tomato Sauce (page 69)

Olive oil spray

1 (1-pound) package store-bought pizza dough, at room temperature

Heat a 10-inch sauté pan over medium heat. Add the sausage and brown it well in its own fat. If the sausage is too lean, add a little olive oil to the pan. Use a slotted spoon and transfer the browned meat to a dish. Drain off all but 1 tablespoon of the fat in the pan. Add the peppers, garlic, and onion and cook over medium heat just until they soften, about 4 minutes. Return the sausage to the pan and stir in the fennel seeds, cheese, salt, pepper, and tomato sauce. Allow the mixture to cool for 10 minutes.

Preheat the oven to 375°F. Lightly spray 2 baking sheets with olive oil and set aside.

Knead the dough on a floured board for a minute or two. Divide it into 8 pieces. Roll each piece into a 7-inch circle. Divide and place some of the filling on half of each circle. Fold the other half over the filling and seal the edges with a fork. Place 4 calzones on each baking sheet, spacing them 2 inches apart.

With a scissors make an x in the center of each calzone. Cover the baking sheets with clean towels and allow the calzones to rise for 20 minutes.

Bake the calzones 20 to 25 minutes or until they are nicely browned on top and bottom. Serve warm.

Note: *To make them ahead of time, allow them to rise as directed and then place the sheets in the freezer until the calzones harden. Wrap each one individually in aluminum foil and pop them into a zip-lock bag. When ready to bake, simply take out what you need. They will take about 5 minutes longer to bake.*

Variation: Cut the dough into 24 pieces and make mini calzones for a buffet party. Bake for 15 minutes.

Panino Favorito della Mamma
Mom's Favorite Chicken Cutlet and Broccoli Rabe Sandwich

A thin, crisp chicken cutlet topped with sautéed broccoli rabe and nestled between two slices of grainy, toasted bread is as Italian as any posh *panino* gets. This is my mother's favorite sandwich, and mine too. It is a satisfying diversion from the more predictable lunchtime sandwiches like ham and cheese and can quickly turn itself into a supper entrée when paired with a green salad and a glass of pinot grigio. It can also be served without the bread, in which case I would definitely add a slice of melted provolone cheese over the top. With or without the bread, this is a winner and a good way to use leftover chicken cutlets, too!

🕐 **Saving time:** Keep a container of toasted bread crumbs in the refrigerator. Use Egg Beaters instead of eggs and buy thinly sliced cutlets.

Serves 4

4 tablespoons extra-virgin olive oil

1 small onion, peeled and diced

1 pound broccoli rabe, stemmed, rinsed, dried, and cut into 2-inch pieces

¼ teaspoon hot red pepper flakes

½ teaspoon fine sea salt

Coarse black pepper to taste

6 oil-cured black olives, pitted and diced (optional)

⅓ cup unbleached all-purpose flour

4 thin slices of chicken cutlets (1 pound)

1 large egg, slightly beaten, or ¼ cup Egg Beaters equivalent

½ cup toasted bread crumbs

8 slices good-quality toasted bread

4 slices provolone cheese (optional)

Heat 2 tablespoons of the olive oil in a 10-inch sauté pan. Stir in the onion and cook until softened. Stir in the broccoli rabe and pepper flakes. Cover the pan and cook over medium heat for 2 or 3 minutes or until the broccoli rabe wilts. Season with ¼ teaspoon of the salt and pepper to taste. Transfer the broccoli rabe to a small bowl. Stir in the olives. Cover and keep warm. Wipe out the pan and return it to the stove.

Pour the flour into a paper bag with the remaining ¼ teaspoon salt and pepper to taste. Dredge each cutlet in the flour and transfer it to a plate. Coat each cutlet with the egg wash; then completely coat it in bread crumbs. Place the cutlets on a baking sheet and set aside.

Heat the remaining oil in the pan and when it is hot, brown the cutlets quickly on each side. Transfer them to a dish as they cook.

Top each of 4 bread slices with a cutlet and spread the broccoli rabe on top of each. If you wish, top the broccoli rabe with slices of provolone cheese and run each under the broiler to melt the cheese. Or just top with the remaining bread slices. Cut the sandwiches in half and serve.

Indulge in a total sandwich experience.

Ciabatta con Salame e Parmigiano-Reggiano
Flat Bread with Salami and Parmesan Cheese

Tomie dePaola comes to my television kitchen often. He has written hundreds of children's books, many of them dealing with Italian food. He also loves to make regional Italian breads. So it is no surprise that his favorite sandwich is made with *ciabatta* bread, a flat bread with a chewy crust and an open-textured crumb. *Ciabatta* is easily found in grocery store bakeries or in Italian bakeries. Use a cheese slicer to make thin slices of Parmigiano-Reggiano cheese.

Serves 4

8 horizontal-cut slices ciabatta or similar country-style bread
Fruity extra-virgin olive oil
16 very thin slices good imported salami
8 slices Parmigiano-Reggiano cheese

Place 1 slice of bread on each of 4 sandwich plates. Drizzle each slice with a little olive oil. Overlap 4 slices of salami over each slice and drizzle a little oil over the top of the salami. Top with a cheese slice and drizzle with a little more oil. Cover with the remaining bread slices.

Mozzarella in Carrozza (Fried Mozzarella Sandwiches)

Zuppa di Pollo Fine Settimana (Weekend Chicken Soup)

Fusilli con Ragù d'Agnello alla Molisana (Corkscrew Macaroni with Lamb Ragù, Molise Style)

Pronto Pollo alla Cacciatore (Quick Hunter-Style Chicken)

Insalata Rinforzata (Sicilian Cauliflower Salad)

Pomodorini con Porri e Timo (Cherry Tomatoes with Leeks and Thyme)

Semifreddo di Limone alla Cinzia (Cindy's Lemon Semifreddo)

Panettone con Spumone (Spumone-Filled Panettone)

Panini di Scamorza, Peperoni e Carciofi
Scamorza Cheese, Sweet Peppers, and Artichoke Sandwiches

Scamorza, a cow's milk cheese made in Molise, is most often eaten as a table cheese but it is great as a sandwich. Look for *scamorza* in the cheese case of your grocery store. For an antipasto, cut the sandwiches into quarters.

Serves 4

---

8 slices sourdough-type bread, toasted

1 pound scamorza cheese, smoked or unsmoked, cut into 8 slices

2 whole marinated sweet red peppers, cut into 4 pieces

4 marinated artichokes, drained and finely chopped

Place 2 slices of scamorza on each of 4 bread slices. Top each with a pepper slice and divide and spread the artichokes over the peppers. Top each with the remaining slices of bread. Cut each sandwich in half and serve.

Variation: Melt slices of scamorza in a small nonstick sauté pan. Sprinkle the slices with a little white vinegar before transferring them to bread slices.

Pizza Margherita
Classic Pizza with Fresh Tomatoes, Mozzarella, and Basil

Pizza is one of my favorite foods and it certainly is fun to make with the whole family. Why not start a tradition in your house and designate Friday or Saturday as pizza night? Your family will look forward to it; it will get them enthusiastic about being in the kitchen and cooking something they love. With pizza for supper, you can plan ahead, and at the same time teach children cooking skills. And you can teach them that pizza can be a good food if made properly. For me the best day of the week is Saturday, when I can prepare Basic Yeast Dough (page 137) either by hand or in a food processor. If saving time is really critical, create your own signature pizza with store-bought dough. If your refrigerator contains mozzarella cheese, tomatoes, and fresh basil, you have the makings of a classic Margherita pizza. Keep anchovies, olives in oil, and oregano at the ready and change it to a Sicilian-style pizza. Or be creative with thin slices of zucchini, prosciutto, and mushrooms. Or make a *scamorza* cheese and *pancetta* pizza. How about potato and caramelized onion pizza?

Serves 4

---

1 recipe Basic Yeast Dough (page 137) or 1 (1-pound) package
　store-bought pizza dough
2 tablespoons extra-virgin olive oil
3 medium plum tomatoes, thinly sliced
1 (8-ounce) ball mozzarella (fior di latte) cheese, cut into small pieces
Salt to taste
4 or 5 basil leaves, torn into small pieces

Preheat the oven to 400°F.

Roll the dough out on a floured surface to a 13-inch round. Place it on a lightly oiled pizza pan. Brush the dough with 1 tablespoon of the oil. Fill the top with the tomato slices. Sprinkle the cheese evenly over the tomatoes. Drizzle with the remaining olive oil. Sprinkle with salt.

Bake the pizza until the edges begin to brown slightly and the underside is nicely browned. Remove the pizza from the oven; let it cool slightly, then cut into wedges with kitchen scissors. Sprinkle the basil over the slices and serve. Now that is true pizza!

Variation: Divide the dough into quarters and make mini pizzas, known as *pizzette*.

PRONTO PIZZA POINTERS

Pizza, along with pasta, is without a doubt a ubiquitous Italian food. It is one of those comfort foods at the top of everyone's crave list. Pizza is the perfect choice for an impromptu party, an easy supper, or a tailgate event, and for most people it is usually a phone call away. But the best pizza is made in your own kitchen and with very little effort. Start with store-bought dough or make your own quickly in a food processor, using the easy recipe on page 137, and you'll get exactly the pizza you want.

I like to bake pizza on a preheated pizza stone that fits in the oven. These stones are unglazed clay slabs and are readily available in kitchen stores. Using them results in an evenly baked pizza with a very crispy crust. Another way to use the stone is to put it on a gas grill and preheat it; then simply slide the prepared pizza onto the stone from a pizza peel or the back of a rimless baking sheet that has been lined with parchment paper. Close the grill top and in about 10 minutes or less, a perfect pizza is ready. Slide the peel or the baking sheet under the parchment paper to lift the pizza off the grill.

Parchment paper is another great cooking tool. You will find it in the aisle with the wax paper and aluminum foil. I roll pizza dough right on it and transfer it to the pizza peel.

It makes it so easy. If you don't have parchment paper, lightly spray pizza pans before transferring the rolled dough onto them. The best pizza pans are about 13 inches in diameter and are perforated with little holes. This allows for even heat and an unsoggy crust.

Need to make pizza ahead of time? Simply make, roll, and spread the dough on pizza pans. Spread toppings. Cover the pizza with plastic wrap and then wrap the pan in aluminum foil and place the whole thing in the freezer. It will keep for several weeks, even up to a month. When that craving hits, or company is due, remove the aluminum foil and plastic wrap. Bake the pizza, frozen, in a preheated 425°F. oven for about 25 to 30 minutes, or until the bottom is crusty and the edges are browned.

The best way to cut pizza is with kitchen scissors.

Polenta

Cooked Cornmeal

Polenta is ground corn (cornmeal) that is cooked in water or milk. It has been a staple in the Italian kitchen for centuries. Once considered a lowly food of the poor, it has claimed its place on chic restaurant menus. Northern Italians prefer to use cornmeal made from a special variety known as Marano, a brilliant orange corn (*mais*) with small hard kernels. When it is cooked it becomes a thick paste of great versatility. Use it in place of bread to make a "sandwich" or top it with the Quick Hunter-Style Chicken (page 86) or the Turkey with Tomato and Mozzarella (page 90). Cut it into slices, top it with cheese, and broil it. Make a lasagne, layering slices with tomato sauce. Coarse- and fine-grind cornmeals are available in grocery and specialty stores. If you want to make it from scratch, prepare to spend about 40 minutes stirring away, but why not make it ahead and refrigerate it? It will last over a week. Really pressed for time? Already cooked polenta is available in cylinder rolls in grocery and specialty stores.

Serves 8 to 10

4½ cups water or chicken or vegetable broth
1 tablespoon salt
1½ cups coarse-ground cornmeal

Use a heavy-duty 4-quart pot so that the cornmeal cooks evenly and with lots of residual heat from the pot.

Pour the water or broth into the pot and stir in the salt and cornmeal. Use a wooden spoon to stir the ingredients well. Put the pot over medium heat and cook, stirring constantly in one direction, until the mixture starts to bubble. Be careful of splatters. As soon as the mixture begins to leave the sides of the pan, pour the polenta out onto an oiled baking sheet or marble board. Spread it thickly into an oblong loaf. Allow it to cool if cutting into slices. Refrigerate it on the baking sheet to speed the cooling. Cut into slices with a knife. Polenta slices can be fried in a little butter or olive oil.

Rotolo di Broccoletto
Stuffed Broccoli Rabe Roll

Store-bought pizza dough can be a blank canvas for so many toppings, but have you ever thought about turning it into a rotolo? Think of this as a large jelly roll stuffed with broccoli rabe and cheese and baked. It makes a great centerpiece for a buffet, or slice it thick and serve it with soup for a weekend supper, or on its own for lunch. Substitute spinach or broccoli for the broccoli rabe, which has more leaves and fewer florets than broccoli. Try your hand at making the dough from scratch; it is quick and easy to do in a food processor. See Basic Yeast Dough, page 137.

Saving time: Use frozen spinach or broccoli instead of fresh. Keep several packages of prepared pizza dough in the freezer.

Serves 8

¼ cup extra-virgin olive oil

2 garlic cloves, peeled and minced

2 pounds fresh broccoli rabe, or 2 packages frozen and defrosted chopped broccoli or spinach

2 tablespoons red wine vinegar

2 tablespoons minced fresh basil

1¼ teaspoons dried oregano

1 teaspoon salt

1 (1 pound) package store-bought pizza dough

1 small ball (4 ounces) mozzarella (fior di latte) cheese, cut into small pieces

¼ pound provolone cheese, cut into small pieces

1 large egg

1 teaspoon water
Coarse salt
Sesame seeds

Heat 3 tablespoons of the oil in a sauté pan and cook the garlic until very soft. Stir in the broccoli rabe or the broccoli or spinach and cook for 3 minutes. Stir in the wine vinegar, basil, oregano, and salt. Transfer the mixture to bowl. Let cool 5 minutes.

Put the dough in a bowl and allow it to come to room temperature. Roll it out on a floured surface into a 12 × 14-inch rectangle and place it on a lightly greased rimless baking sheet. Don't worry if it does not fit, since you are going to roll the dough up.

Brush the top of the dough with the remaining olive oil. Spread the broccoli mixture over the top to within ½ inch of the edges. Scatter the cheeses on top.

Starting with the side closest to you, roll the dough up tightly like a jelly roll on the baking sheet, tucking in the 2 side ends as you roll. Pinch the undersides of the dough together to seal it.

Mix the egg with the water in a small bowl and use it to brush the top of the dough. Then sprinkle the coarse salt and sesame seeds evenly over the top.

Preheat the oven to 375°F.

Cover the roll with a towel and allow it to rise for 25 minutes. Bake for 30 to 35 minutes or until nicely browned. Let the roll cool about 5 minutes on the baking sheet before using a large spatula to transfer it to a cooling rack.

Cut the roll while warm into thick slices.

Pronto Desserts

Ricotta con Miele e Mandorle (Ricotta with Honey and Almonds)

Biscotti di Cioccolato e Noci (Chocolate and Walnut Biscotti)

Crema della Mamma (Mom's Velvety Custard)

Fichi Secchi al Vino Rosso (Dried Figs in Red Wine)

Frutta in Sciroppo (Poached Fruit)

Gelato con Fragole, Pesce e Aceto Balsamico (Ice Cream Sundae with Strawberries,
    Peaches, and Balsamic Vinegar)

Meringhe (Puffy Meringues)

Pere Cotte con Albiccoche e Vino (Baked Pears with Dried Apricots and Wine)

Semifreddo di Limone alla Cinzia (Cindy's Lemon Semifreddo)

Panettone con Spumone (Spumone-Filled Panettone)

Taralli Dolci con Anice (Sweet Anise Taralli)

Torta Cioccolatini alla Cristiana (Cristiana's Chocolate "Candy" Flourless Cake)

Torta di Mela e Panna (Apple Cream Tart)

Tortine Dolci con Mascarpone, Lamponi e Cioccolata (Little Sweet Tarts with
    Mascarpone, Raspberries, and Chocolate)

Torta di Gelato (Ice Cream Pie)

There are those among us who believe that no meal is complete without dessert, what the Italians call *dolce*. This usually means an exotic multiflavored scoop of gelato towering out of a cup or cone that one enjoys while strolling in the piazza; it could also mean something more predictable like *frutta fresca,* fresh fruit. The real stars of the Italian sweet world are glistening fruit tarts, liqueur-soaked cakes, and dainty cookies, which are always present for special occasions. Rarely are *dolci* made at home anymore in Italy, but that should not stop you from trying the showstoppers in this chapter. They are effortless to prepare and a joy to eat.

Ricotta con Miele e Mandorle
Ricotta with Honey and Almonds

Ricotta for dessert? Now that's very Italian, and so dramatic when it is served with a drizzle of warm honey and sprinkled with sliced almonds. Try it with good marmalades, too, like orange or blueberry. Success depends on one thing—the quality of the ricotta. Whole-milk ricotta is richer-tasting, but skim will work well, too. Be sure to drain it well in a colander so that it is solid and not weeping with water. There are many pasteurized brands in supermarkets, but if you can get fresh ricotta from an Italian specialty store, you will recognize immediately the difference in taste. This is a classic dessert for any occasion.

Serves 4

---

1 pound whole-milk ricotta, well drained
½ cup honey
½ cup sliced almonds

Divide the cheese among 4 dessert plates. Warm the honey in a small saucepan or in the microwave for 10 seconds. Drizzle 2 tablespoons over the top of each plate and sprinkle with some of the almonds. Serve.

Variation: For a more elegant presentation, use 4-ounce ramekins. Line them with plastic wrap, allowing for an overhang. Divide the cheese among the ramekins and be sure to spread it evenly. Invert each ramekin onto a dessert plate and carefully peel away the plastic wrap. Drizzle on the honey, sprinkle with the almonds, and serve.

Biscotti di Cioccolato e Noci
Chocolate and Walnut Biscotti

Let me introduce you to a 1-bowl biscotti that is one of my favorites. The dough is filled with chopped milk chocolate and walnuts and is so quick to make. These biscotti are always in my freezer and on my list of must-make cookies for the holidays.

🕐 **Saving time:** Buy the walnuts pre-chopped; make the dough ahead of time and refrigerate it for up to 3 days.

Makes about 3 dozen

½ cup unsalted butter, softened

¾ cup sugar

2 large eggs

1 tablespoon vanilla extract

2 cups unbleached all-purpose flour

1½ teaspoons baking powder

½ teaspoon salt

4 ounces good quality milk chocolate (such as Callebaut), coarsely chopped

1 cup chopped walnuts

Preheat the oven to 325°F.

Line 2 baking sheets with parchment paper and set aside.

Whisk the butter and sugar together in a large bowl until light and fluffy. Whisk in the eggs, 1 at a time, and blend well. Whisk in the vanilla.

Using a wooden spoon, mix in the flour, baking powder, and salt. Mix well. Stir in the chocolate and walnuts.

Divide the dough and transfer half to each baking sheet. Flour your hands and pat the dough into a loaf about 12 inches long and 4 inches wide.

Bake the loaves for 25 minutes, or until they are firm to the touch and lightly browned. Carefully transfer them to a cutting board and allow them to cool about 5 minutes. Using a sharp knife, cut ½-inch-thick diagonal slices from each loaf. Return the slices to the baking sheets and bake an additional 10 minutes, or until they are dry and nicely browned.

Transfer the biscotti to cooling racks. Store in an airtight container or freeze.

Crema della Mamma
Mom's Velvety Custard

Soothing vanilla bean–infused egg custard with a lush velvet texture is one of those comfort foods from home that I make often. The dessert has an ancient history dating from the sixth century. Then it was sweetened with honey, not sugar. This custard has character and can stand on its own, but it can be dressed up for entertaining with the fresh Poached Fruit on page 162. Elegant to look at and fun to eat, it can be made a day ahead. Baking the custard in a water bath ensures even heat and a creamy consistency.

Makes six ½-cup servings

Butter spray
4 large eggs, lightly beaten
2 cups milk
1 cup nonfat half-and-half
½ cup sugar
2-inch piece of vanilla bean, slit
½ teaspoon salt

Preheat the oven to 350°F.

Lightly spray 6 custard cups (3 × 1½ inches) with butter spray and place them in a baking pan large enough to hold them with space between each one. Set aside.

Lightly whisk the eggs together in a 2-quart bowl with a pourable spout, if possible. Set aside.

Pour the milk and half-and-half into a 1-quart saucepan. Stir in the sugar. Scrape the seeds from the vanilla bean into the pot and add the bean and salt. Bring the milk mixture to just under the boil. With a spoon remove the vanilla bean. (Dry the bean and save it for another use.)

Whisk 1 cup of the milk mixture into the eggs. Then whisk in the remaining milk mixture.

Divide and pour the mixture among the custard cups. Pour hot water carefully three-quarters of the way up the side of the baking pan, being careful not to get water into the custard cups. Bake for 30 to 35 minutes, or just until a knife inserted in the center comes out clean. Remove the cups from the baking pan and allow them to cool on a rack for 10 minutes. Refrigerate, covered, until ready to use.

Serve as is with sliced fruit or berries on top or run a knife around the inside edge of the cups and unmold each one onto a dessert dish. Serve with Poached Fruit (page 162).

Fichi Secchi al Vino Rosso
Dried Figs in Red Wine

A bowl full of fresh figs always makes a statement on Italian tables. Figs are a fruit with biblical and historic significance. With their plump form and intense, sweet flavor, there is little that can match their taste. And when they vanish with the season, I resort to dried figs cooked in red wine as a savory stand-in. Find dried figs in the baking aisle of your grocery store.

Serves 4

1 teaspoon butter
12 large Calimyrna figs
⅓ cup chopped walnuts
1 cup dry red wine
¼ cup honey
1 tablespoon grated orange zest

Preheat the oven to 350°F.

Lightly grease a small dutch oven–type casserole dish (about 6 inches in diameter) or a soufflé dish with the butter.

Make a small incision with a knife at the bottom of each fig to form a small hole. Divide and stuff some of the walnuts into the hole of each fig and place the figs stem side up in a single layer in the casserole dish.

Heat the wine and honey in a small pot until the honey dissolves. Pour the mixture over the figs. Sprinkle the zest over the figs, cover the casserole, and bake for 25 minutes.

Allow the figs to cool to room temperature.

To serve, place 3 figs on each of 4 dessert dishes and pour some of the wine sauce over them.

Frutta in Sciroppo
Poached Fruit

Macedonia is the traditional "fruit cocktail" of Italy, usually offered as dessert and served with gelato. I prefer to serve gelato with this versatile poached fresh fruit sauce. I love it over Mom's Velvety Custard, too (page 158). This is the perfect summertime dessert and everything can be made a day or two in advance.

🕐 **Saving time:** Use 1½ cups mixed dried fruits in place of fresh.

Serves 6

¾ **cup sugar**
¾ **cup dry white wine such as chardonnay, pinot grigio, or apiane**
2 yellow or white peaches, washed, cut in half, pitted, and sliced ¼ inch thick
2 nectarines, washed, cut in half, pitted, and sliced ¼ inch thick

For Serving

Pistachio ice cream
8 whole cherries on stems
Mint sprigs for garnish

Combine the sugar and wine in a 1-quart saucepan over medium heat. Cook, stirring, until the mixture begins to thicken slightly. Stir in the peaches and nectarines and cook for 2 or 3 minutes or just until the fruits begin to soften. Do not allow them to get mushy. If using dried fruits, cook about 5 minutes or just until they soften.

Transfer the fruit with the syrup to a bowl. Cover and refrigerate at least 1 hour.

Spoon the fruit with some of the syrup into each of 4 dessert bowls or goblets and top with a scoop of pistachio ice cream. Garnish each dish with 2 cherries and a mint sprig.

Gelato con Fragole, Pesce e Aceto Balsamico
Ice Cream Sundae with Strawberries, Peaches, and Balsamic Vinegar

Ever since balsamic vinegar appeared on the American food scene, cooks have been using it to embellish the taste of salads, cooked meats, and marinades. But did you know that one of the favorite ways to have it in Italy is over ice cream? True balsamic vinegar (*aceto balsamico tradizionale*) is, at a bare minimum, aged for twelve years, but can be much older and syrupy in texture with the rich taste of a good port. Commercially prepared balsamic vinegar (*aceto balsamico commerciale*) from the grocery store is not the same thing; this is mainly red wine vinegar with a little balsamic thrown in. So for this ice cream and fresh fruit balsamic vinegar "sundae," use the real thing, which is available at Italian specialty food stores and from food catalogues. It is pricey, but a little goes a very long way. This is a wonderful company dessert that takes only minutes to make and can be made ahead.

Serves 4

---

2 cups sliced fresh strawberries
2 large white or yellow peaches, peeled and sliced
1 tablespoon lemon juice
5 tablespoons honey
1 tablespoon balsamic vinegar
1 pint vanilla ice cream
Mint sprigs for garnish

Combine the strawberries, peaches, and lemon juice in a bowl. Whisk the honey and balsamic vinegar together in a small bowl, then pour the mixture over the fruits and gently coat them with a spoon. Cover and allow the fruits to marinate at least 1 hour.

Meanwhile, scoop ice cream into each of 4 ice cream dishes or wineglasses. Cover each one with plastic wrap and place them in the freezer.

When ready to serve, remove the ice cream dishes from the freezer and top each one with some of the fruit sauce. Garnish with a mint sprig. Serve immediately.

Meringhe
Puffy Meringues

Got egg whites? Meringues are the easiest and most exotic cookie to make with left-over egg whites, or if you want to start from scratch, with fresh eggs or powdered egg whites. *Meringhe* are an Italian favorite, and big, wispy puffs of them are always piled high in pastry shop windows. They can be flavored with extracts, citrus zests, chopped nuts, chocolate, and dried fruits. They are a special treat for children when formed into cream-puff sizes and served with a scoop of ice cream, and are a wonderful addition to a dinner party when served with a fresh berry sauce. The best part is that they are fast to make, and once they're in the oven you can almost forget about them.

Makes about 6 dozen

---

4 large egg whites
¼ teaspoon salt
½ teaspoon cream of tartar
1 cup sugar
1 tablespoon almond extract
1 teaspoon white vinegar

Preheat the oven to 250°F.

Use a stand mixer to beat the whites on medium speed until they are foamy. Add salt and cream of tartar, increase the speed to high, and slowly pour in the sugar while beating, along with the extract and vinegar. Beat until the whites are very stiff and shiny.

Line two baking sheets with parchment paper. Using a pastry bag fitted with a star tip, fill the bag half full with the meringue and pipe out 1-inch drops, spacing them a little apart. Or use 2 teaspoons to drop about a tablespoon-size amount onto the baking sheets.

Bake the meringues for 25 to 30 minutes. Do not open the oven while they are baking. Turn off the oven and allow them to remain in the oven for 1 hour. Remove the baking sheets and let the meringues cool before transferring them to a cooling rack.

Variations: Fold nuts, chocolate, dried fruits, toffee, crushed peppermint candy, or other favorites into the meringue after it is beaten to stiff peaks.

Pere Cotte con Albiccoche e Vino
Baked Pears with Dried Apricots and Wine

Pears are the quintessential Italian dessert, usually served with cheese. Baked pears in wine is also a popular dish. Here they are treated to a more upscale presentation with a filling of apricots and marmalade to complement the flavor of the pears. Cooking them in the microwave is fast. Although the dessert takes minimal effort to prepare, it looks as if time was spent in the kitchen.

Serves 4

---

8 dried California apricots, diced

2 Anjou, Bartlett, or Packham pears, cut in half lengthwise and core removed

2 teaspoons orange marmalade

1 tablespoon unsalted butter, cut into 4 pieces

1 cup dessert wine such as moscato

4 tablespoons ricotta cheese

1 tablespoon sugar

¼ cup coarsely chopped walnuts

Mint leaves for garnish

Place the apricots in a small saucepan and pour in just enough water to cover them. Bring the water to a boil, lower the heat, and cook for 2 minutes. Drain the apricots and transfer them to a small bowl. Stir in the marmalade.

Place the pear halves in each of 4 individual microwave-proof bowls. Fill the cavities of each pear half with some of the apricot mixture. Dot the tops of each with a piece of butter.

Carefully pour ¼ cup of the wine along the sides of each bowl. Cover each bowl with a sheet of wax paper.

Microwave the pears on high power for 5 to 6 minutes or just until they are soft but not mushy. Allow the pears to cool to room temperature.

In a small bowl beat the ricotta cheese with the sugar. Place a tablespoon of cheese on top of each pear half. Divide and sprinkle the nuts on top. Add a mint leaf for garnish and serve.

Semifreddo di Limone alla Cinzia
Cindy's Lemon Semifreddo

Even pastry chefs like to save time in the kitchen, like chef Cindy Salvato, who is also the food stylist on the television series *Ciao Italia*. Her smooth and cool *Semifreddo di Limone*, partially frozen lemon dessert, is tangy and zesty with a rich, creamy texture and can be made days ahead. Serve it with Cindy's Blueberry Compote, which can also be made ahead. As an added bonus, Cindy says it can be served unfrozen as a mousse in tall goblets or as a filling for sponge cake or cream puffs.

🕐 **Saving time:** For recipes calling for citrus juice, buy several lemons, limes, or oranges. Squeeze and freeze the juice in ice cube trays for future use.

Serves 6

---

5 large eggs
1 cup granulated sugar
1 stick unsalted butter, melted
1 cup fresh-squeezed lemon juice
2 cups heavy cream
½ cup coarsely ground pistachio nuts

Line a 4 × 8-inch loaf pan with plastic wrap and set aside.

Whip the eggs and sugar in a bowl on high speed with an electric mixer until the mixture triples in bulk. Set the mixer on low speed and slowly add the melted butter. Add the lemon juice. The batter will deflate some. Don't worry.

Transfer the mixture to the top of a double boiler and cook over boiling water until thickened, whisking constantly. The mixture should be the consistency of loose pudding. Remove from the heat; transfer the mixture to a bowl. Cover with plastic wrap and cool completely in the refrigerator.

Whip the cream to soft peaks and fold it into the cooled lemon mixture. Pour it into the loaf pan and spread it evenly. Completely cover the top with nuts. Cover the pan and freeze.

To serve, remove the semifreddo from the pan by lifting it out with the plastic wrap or turn it upside down to unmold it. Unwrap the semifreddo and place it nut side down on a cutting board. Cut the loaf into 1-inch slices. Place a slice on individual dessert plates. Serve with blueberry compote.

Cindy's Blueberry Compote

⅓ cup brown sugar
1 tablespoon cornstarch
½ cup water
1 vanilla bean, split lengthwise, seeds scraped
1 tablespoon limoncello liqueur or lemon juice
3 cups fresh blueberries

Combine the sugar, cornstarch, water, vanilla bean seeds (reserve the bean pod for another use), and limoncello in a saucepan. Stir in the berries and cook them over low heat, stirring gently, until the berries are translucent. Remove from the heat and cool.

Note: *Make vanilla-flavored sugar with the vanilla bean pod. Simply store the pod with sugar in a tightly closed container.*

Panettone con Spumone
Spumone-Filled Panettone

Panettone with ice cream is an impressive no-cook, do-ahead dessert that is as much fun to make as to eat. This tall, sweet, raised bread with citron and raisins used to be available only at holiday time, but is now found year-round in supermarkets and Italian food stores. This is a good way to use up *panettone* if you received one too many for Christmas!

Saving time: Thaw the ice cream in the microwave for 20 seconds.

Serves 8 to 10

---

1 store-bought panettone
1½ quarts spumone ice cream or your favorite flavor ice cream, softened
Whipped cream, optional

Cut a 1-inch-thick slice off the top of the bread and set it aside. Use a bread knife to cut around the inside of the bread and hollow it out, leaving a ½-inch-thick base and wall. (Save the bread pieces to make bread pudding.)

Fill the panettone with ice cream, packing it in firmly. Replace the top. Wrap the bread in aluminum foil and freeze until ready to serve. Allow the panettone to thaw slightly before cutting it into wedges or rounds. Serve with whipped cream or raspberry sauce, page 173.

Raspberry Sauce

1 pint raspberries, washed and drained
3 tablespoons sugar
1 teaspoon fresh lemon juice

Puree or mash the berries. Sieve the berries through a strainer into a small bowl.
Stir in the sugar and lemon juice. Drizzle a little of the sauce on individual servings.

Taralli Dolci con Anice
Sweet Anise Taralli

Dry biscuits known as *taralli* (little round things) are always present at mealtime on southern Italian tables. Depending on where you are in Italy, they can be made with yeast dough and flavored with hot red pepper and coarse black pepper. They can be tamer-tasting when left just plain, or they can be turned into a sweet little something like this nonyeast cookie version flavored with honey, anise extract, and anise seeds and dipped in a confectioners' glaze. The dough is quick to make in a food processor or a stand mixer.

Saving time: Make the dough ahead, wrap it, and refrigerate it for up to 2 days.

Makes 36 twists

Dough

4 extra-large eggs
½ cup extra-virgin olive oil
1½ teaspoons anise extract
1 tablespoon anise seeds, ground
½ cup honey
4 to 4½ cups unbleached all-purpose flour
½ teaspoon fine sea salt
2 tablespoons baking powder

Confectioners' Glaze

1½ cups confectioners' sugar
3 to 4 tablespoons half-and-half or milk

Preheat the oven to 350°F.

Line 2 baking sheets with parchment paper and set aside.

Whirl the eggs in a food processor or blend them in a stand mixer until fluffy. Add the olive oil, anise extract, anise seeds, and honey and whirl or blend the ingredients.

Combine 4 cups of the flour, the salt, and baking powder in a bowl. Slowly add the mixture to the food processor or mixer and process or mix to form a soft dough; it should be the consistency of Play-Doh. If more flour is needed add it 1 tablespoon at a time.

Knead the dough on a work surface to smooth it. Divide the dough into 4 equal pieces and work with 1 at a time; keep the rest under damp paper towels.

Roll each piece into an 18-inch rope and cut eighteen 1-inch pieces from each rope.

Roll each of 2 pieces into an 8-inch rope. Attach the two pieces at one end and twist them together. Bring the 2 ends together and pinch them closed to make a small circle.

Place the taralli on the baking sheets, spacing them 1 inch apart.

Bake the taralli for 15 to 20 minutes or until nicely browned. While the taralli bake, make the glaze: In a bowl, combine the sugar and the half-and-half.

Remove the taralli from the baking sheets and, while they are still warm, dip the tops of each one in the confectioners' sugar glaze and place on a cooling rack to dry completely. Store in an airtight container.

Torta Cioccolatini alla Cristiana

Cristiana's Chocolate "Candy" Flourless Cake

Cristiana Magnani is a friend who lives in Reggio Emilia. To relieve the stress of her life as a neonatologist (a doctor who treats premature babies), she bakes. By her own admission she has a huge sweet tooth. One of her favorite creations is this *Torta Cioccolatini*, a flourless cake that tastes like rich chocolate candy, as its name implies. Cristiana says this cake is always ready in the freezer for herself and unexpected guests. The cake has a frozen shelf life of a month, defrosts in 20 minutes, and is easily put together from ingredients already on hand. Truly, it is like eating a fudgy chocolate bar.

Makes one 10-inch cake

1 sheet dampened parchment paper large enough to overhang the pan
1 stick plus 1 tablespoon unsalted butter
7 ounces bittersweet chocolate, cut into small pieces
1 cup sugar
4 large eggs, separated
1 tablespoon vanilla extract
Confectioners' sugar for garnish

Spray a 10-inch cake pan with baking spray. Line the pan with the parchment paper, allowing an excess to overhang the sides of the pan. This will make it easy to lift the cake out of the pan after it is baked.

Melt the butter in a small saucepan or in the microwave for 20 seconds. Off the heat stir in the chocolate and set aside.

Beat the sugar with the egg yolks in a large bowl with a hand-held mixer until the mixture is light and lemon colored. Combine the chocolate and sugar mixture. Stir in the vanilla and set aside.

Beat the whites in a clean bowl with clean beaters until soft peaks form; do not overbeat or the whites will be too dry, making it hard to fold them into the chocolate mixture. Fold one-third of the whites into the chocolate. Then fold in the remainder, taking care to do this gently so as not to deflate the batter.

Scrape the batter into the prepared pan and place it in a cold oven. Turn the oven on to 350°F and bake 20 minutes or just until the cake is set; it should remain moist. Remove the cake and cool it in the pan at room temperature for 20 minutes.

Refrigerate the cake until ready to serve. Carefully lift the cake out of the pan with the parchment paper. Cut around the parchment paper with a scissors or carefully remove the paper and discard it.

Place the cake on a cake dish. Sprinkle the top with confectioners' sugar and cut it into thin wedges. It melt in your mouth.

Note: *If making the cake to freeze for future use, do not sprinkle it with confectioners' sugar until ready to serve.*

Torta di Mela e Panna
Apple Cream Tart

Yellow Golden Delicious apple trees dot the countryside of the region of Emilia-Romagna. These apples are ideal for this dreamy apple cream tart. The crust is made in 3 minutes in a food processor, then patted into a pan. No struggling with rolling out pastry dough. While it bakes, the tart smells divine as the intoxicating aromas of cinnamon and cloves perfume the kitchen. Serve it warm with a little vanilla ice cream or a dollop of smooth mascarpone cheese.

🕐 **Saving time:** The easy pat-into-a-pan crust can be assembled ahead of time and either refrigerated or frozen until needed.

Makes one 9- or 10-inch tart

Crust

2 cups unbleached all-purpose flour
2 tablespoons sugar
½ teaspoon salt
¼ teaspoon baking powder
½ cup cold butter, cut into bits

Filling

3 medium-size Golden Delicious apples, peeled and thinly sliced
⅔ cup sugar

½ teaspoon cinnamon

¼ teaspoon cloves

¼ teaspoon nutmeg

2 egg yolks

1 cup heavy cream

Preheat the oven to 400°F.

Combine the flour, sugar, salt, and baking powder in a bowl. Cut in the butter with a pastry blender or fork until the mixture looks like coarse crumbs. Pat the mixture evenly into a 9- or 10-inch greased cake pan. Set aside.

If using a food processor, pulse the flour, sugar, salt, and baking powder together. Add butter and pulse until mixture is coarse.

Arrange the apple slices on the crust in an overlapping pattern, filling in the entire surface.

Combine the sugar, cinnamon, cloves, and nutmeg in a small bowl and sprinkle it evenly over the apple slices.

Bake the tart for 15 minutes.

Meanwhile, whisk the egg yolks in a small bowl with the heavy cream. Pour evenly over the apples and bake 30 minutes longer or until the top is golden brown.

Remove the tart from the oven and cool it on a rack for 10 minutes. Cut into wedges and serve warm.

Variation: I sometimes use Cortland apples, which also make a delicious tart.

Tortine Dolci con Mascarpone, Lamponi e Cioccolata
Little Sweet Tarts with Mascarpone, Raspberries, and Chocolate

These sweet little tarts glisten in every pastry shop window that I have ever drooled over in my travels. Using commercially prepared puff pastry makes *tortine* fun and effortless to make, and the shells can be frozen for up to a month. Bake, cool, and fill up to several hours ahead on the day they are needed. Vary the fruits with the seasons.

Makes 4 to 6 tarts

1 sheet commercially prepared puff pastry, thawed in the refrigerator
Four to six 3⅓ × ¾-inch tart shells with removable bottoms
1 cup mascarpone cheese at room temperature
2 tablespoons confectioners' sugar
2 pints raspberries
4 tablespoons apple jelly, melted
1 small (4-ounce) bar good semisweet chocolate, shaved into curls with a
   vegetable peeler
Mint leaves for garnish

Preheat the oven to 425°F.

Prepare the puff pastry and line the tart shells as described for Little Cheese Tarts (page 26).

Prick each tart shell several times with a fork to prevent them from puffing up in the oven when baked, or place a small sheet of aluminum foil over each tart and spread uncooked rice or dried beans over the top to prevent puffing.

Place the shells on a baking sheet.

Bake for 8 minutes or until nicely browned. Remove the tart shells to a cooling rack. If you used the foil-and-rice method, remove and discard them. Allow the tart shells to cool completely.

In a medium-size bowl beat the cheese with the confectioners' sugar; divide and spread it among the tart shells. Arrange the raspberries on top of the mascarpone to completely cover the top.

Brush the raspberries with the melted apple jelly and scatter some of the chocolate curls over the top. Add a mint leaf.

Refrigerate until ready to serve.

Torta di Gelato
Ice Cream Pie

Save those stale cookies and cake slices! Toast them in the oven, then grind them in a food processor or with a rolling pin and put them in your freezer. They are the perfect instant "crust" for a gelato pie.

Saving time: Soften ice-cream pints in a microwave for 20 seconds. This will make ice cream easy to spread.

Serves 6 to 8

---

3 cups stale plain cookie or cake crumbs
6 tablespoons unsalted butter, melted
1 pint vanilla ice cream (or other flavor)
1 pint chocolate ice cream (or other flavor)

Put the crumbs in a medium-size bowl and pour the butter over them. Mix the crumbs well with your hands to coat them. Reserve ½ cup of the crumbs. Pat the rest evenly in the bottom and partway up the sides of a 9-inch pie plate.

Spread the softened vanilla ice cream over the crumbs. Place the pie in the freezer until the ice cream hardens. Spread the chocolate ice cream over the vanilla. Sprinkle the reserved crumbs over the top. Cover the pie and return to the freezer.

Cut into wedges. Serve as is or with a dollop of sweetened whipped cream.

Pronto Menus

It can be time-consuming to try to put a menu together for every day of the week! You want to be creative but at the same time you want to spend as little time as possible coming up with a manageable scheme, and you don't want to fuss at the end of a busy workday. So you resort to the same old plan that everybody knows by heart and that can lead to an uninteresting meal rut. Monday, it's spaghetti and meatballs, Tuesday, hamburgers, and so on. Sometimes we slip into really dangerous habits when we are too busy to cook, and we bring home fast foods that often only provide lots of fat and calories. But when you plan, you make better, more healthful choices, and your wallet will love it, too, because homemade fast food is so much better and cheaper than what the fast-track, fast-food chains dish up.

The recipes in this book can provide some refreshing menu planning for every day and for company, too. To save you time, I have paired recipes together that I think are complementary to one another. Look them over and mix and match as you see fit. Those recipes marked with an asterisk can be made ahead and stored in the refrigerator or freezer.

Many of the recipes can be used for multiple meal planning; for instance, the dough for *Calzoni Pronti* (page 138) is also great for making pizza, small rolls, a loaf of bread, bread sticks, a two-crusted *pizza rustica* or the *Rotolo di Broccoletto* (page 150). The meatball recipe for *Zuppa di Polpettine* (page 34) can also be used to make larger-size meatballs for spaghetti. Or make them mini size and add them to a baked lasagne or use them as part of an antipasto.

It is this kind of cross-culinary thinking that can make life after five easy. Once you start to cook this way, you will come up with some of your own methods to improvise and maximize meal preparation.

Pronto Menus

Fantastico! An Easy Company Dinner

Little Ciabatta Toasts with Ricotta and Salami (page 16)*
Skillet Breaded Pork Chops with Rosemary (page 78)
Cherry Tomatoes with Leeks and Thyme (page 130)*
Dried Figs in Red Wine (page 160)*

Filling for the toasts can be combined ahead of time and refrigerated. Bread can be presliced. The Cherry Tomatoes with Leeks and Thyme can be made a day ahead and simply reheated in the microwave. Figs can be cooked a day or 2 ahead of time and refrigerated.

* Can be prepared ahead

Kids Cook

Pastina and Egg Soup with Spinach (page 31)
Calzones with Sausage and Peppers (page 138)*
Ice Cream Pie (page 182)*

Calzones prepared with store-bought dough can be made ahead and simply re-heated or frozen for future use. Make the ice-cream pie 2 weeks ahead.

Saturday Night Favorites

Zucchini Soup with Cheese and Eggs (page 30)*
Mom's Favorite Chicken Cutlet and Broccoli Rabe Sandwich (page 140)
Ice Cream Sundae with Strawberries, Peaches, and Balsamic Vinegar (page 164)*

Dice the zucchini 2 days prior and store in a plastic bag in the refrigerator. Clean and cook the broccoli rabe and refrigerate. Make and refrigerate the balsamic vinegar sauce. Clean and slice the fruits; toss them with a little lemon juice and store in a container up to an hour before serving.

Sunday Special

Lazy Lasagne (page 48)*
Caesar Salad (page 112)
Baked Pears with Dried Apricots and Wine (page 168)

Lasagne always tastes better the next day, so make this on Saturday for Sunday, and simply reheat. Double the recipe and freeze one. The pears can be baked ahead and the parmesan wafers made for the salad.

Festive Party Buffet for Six

*Assorted Italian Cheeses and Cured Olives**
Layered Eggplant and Zucchini Casserole (page 126)*
Cubanelle Peppers Stuffed with Rice and Cheese (page 128)*
Neapolitan Potato Pie (page 124)*

Mixed Roasted Vegetable Salad with Scamorza Cheese (page 118)*
Cindy's Lemon Semifreddo (page 170)*

Everything except the potato pie can be prepared a day ahead of time. Make the potato pie early on the day of the party and refrigerate. Bake it just before guests arrive so it is hot. The semifreddo as well as its sauce can be made several days ahead. Bring the cheeses to room temperature an hour before serving. Double the recipes to serve 12.

A Meal in a Pot

Meatball Soup (page 34)*
Neapolitan Stack Salad (page 109)
Sweet Anise Taralli (page 174)*

Hearty Meatball Soup is just the thing to make on the weekend with children. Have them help you form the meatballs. Make it in a Crock-Pot if you have one; make it early, let it simmer, and and forget it. Double the recipe to freeze. Use the same meatball recipe to make larger-size meatballs for spaghetti. Tomatoes and cheese can be sliced several hours ahead and held in plastic containers in the refrigerator. Make the *taralli* cookies ahead and have on hand in the freezer.

Three Easy Plates

Vermicelli Pie Without Eggs (page 50)
Sicilian Cauliflower Salad (page 120)*
Poached Fruit with Ice Cream (page 162)*

The salad can be made hours ahead; the fruit can be made a day ahead and refrigerated.

Something Different

Turkey with Tomato and Mozzarella (page 90)
Polenta (page 148)*
Oven-Roasted Cauliflower (page 122)*
Mom's Velvety Custard (page 158)*

Use already prepared polenta; just slice and sauté it quickly in a little olive oil. The custard can be made a day ahead and refrigerated. The cauliflower can be prepped a day ahead and held in a plastic bag in the refrigerator until ready to roast.

Surprise Package

Steamed Salmon with Vermicelli in Parchment (page 94)*
Fennel, Radicchio, and Orange Salad (page 116)*
Cristiana's Chocolate "Candy" Flourless Cake (page 176)*

Vermicelli can be cooked and refrigerated ahead of time. Salad ingredients can be prepped hours ahead of time and put together at the last minute. Make the cake 2 weeks ahead and freeze.

Friday Night Unwinder

Quick Hunter-Style Chicken (page 86)*
Neapolitan Potato Pie (page 124)*

Green Beans in Tomato Sauce (page 131)*
Ricotta with Honey and Almonds (page 155)

Chicken can be made 2 days ahead. Potatoes can be prepped and held covered in water for a day in the refrigerator. Tomato sauce is already on hand in your refrigerator or freezer, and green beans can be prepped a day ahead.

Special Occasion

Linguine with Lemon and Cream (page 51)
Veal with Gorgonzola Sauce (page 76)
Skillet Tomatoes with Cheese and Bread Crumbs (page 132)*
Little Sweet Tarts with Mascarpone, Raspberries, and Chocolate (page 180)*

Tomatoes can be made 2 hours ahead of time and reheated. Tart shells can be lined with puff pastry 2 days ahead and refrigerated. Bake and fill several hours ahead of time and refrigerate.

Quick Leftover Lunch

Fried Spaghetti Omelet (page 98)
Sliced Tomatoes Drizzled with Olive Oil and Fresh Basil
Fresh Fruit

Leftover pasta in any form is always great reheated and this applies to the spaghetti frittata. Add a few sliced tomatoes and fresh fruit, and a delightful lunch is realized in no time.

Mail Order

Ciao Times
PO Box 891
Durham, New Hampshire 03824
www.ciaoitalia.com
Source for Ciao Italia–related products including DVDs and personalized aprons

Claudio's King of Cheese
929 South Ninth Street
South Philadelphia, Pennsylvania 19147
Olive oils, wide variety of dried pasta, cheeses from most regions of Italy, balsamic vinegars, capers, olives

Colavita USA
2537 Brunswick Avenue
Linden, New Jersey 07036
www.colavita.com
Canned plum tomatoes, vinegars, olive oil, orecchiette and other specialty dried pasta, and specialty food baskets

D. Coluccio & Sons, Inc.
1214 60th Street
Brooklyn, New York 11219
A complete Italian grocery stoe carrying a wide variety of imported Italian food-stuffs from dried beans and lentils to olive oils, cured meats, cheeses, and tuna in olive oil

Dean & DeLuca
Catalog Orders
PO Box 20810
Wichita, Kansas 67208-6810
www.deandeluca.com
Cookware, Italian meats, cheeses, and spices

DiBruno Brothers
109 South 18th Street
Philadelphia, Pennsylvania 19103
(215-665-9220) (Catalog)

Fantes
1006 South 9th Street
Philadelphia, Pennsylvania 19417
(800-878-5557)
www.fantes.com
Large selection of baking needs, cookware, molds, cake pans

Gallucci's Italian Foods
6610 Euclid Avenue
Cleveland, Ohio 44103

(216-881-0045) (Catalog)

A wide variety of cheeses, including *fior di latte*, cured meats, olive oils, wine, pasta flours, nuts, flavorings; an all-encompassing Italian supermarket

Joe Pace and Sons

335 Main Street

Saugus, Massachussets 02113

(781-231-9599)

Quality meats and provisions, well-stocked grocery store, Italian seeds, balsamic vinegars, polenta, rice, tuna in olive oil, capers, Italian cookies, and panettone

King Arthur Flour

PO Box 1010

Norwich, Vermont 05055

(800-827-6836) (Baker's Catalog)

www.kingarthurflour.com

A baker's dream of a store: all types of flour, including Italian flours, dried yeast, extracts, nuts, flavorings, meringue powder, chocolate, and decorative sugars

The Spice Corner

904 South Ninth Street

Philadelphia, Pennsylvania 19147

(800-SPICES) or 215-925-1661

www.thespicecorner.com

Outstanding assortment of dried herbs, spices, coffees, and teas

Venda Ravioli Company
265 Atwells Avenue
Providence, Rhode Island 02903
(401-421-9105)
www.vendaravioli.com
Full line of imported Italian food products including some of the finest olive oils, complete deli department, homemade filled pasta, capers, olives, *ricotta salata* cheese, sea salts, balsamic vinegars, tuna in olive oil, instant polenta, rice, flours, and Italian cooking utensils and ceramic ware

Zabar's
2245 Broadway
New York, New York
(800-697-6301)(Catalog)
www.zabars.com
Cookware, Italian meats, cheeses, and spices

Index